PREPARATION OF INEXPENSIVE
TEACHING MATERIALS

Chandler Publications in

AUDIOVISUAL COMMUNICATIONS

Sidney C. Eboch, **OPERATING AUDIOVISUAL EQUIPMENT**

Jerrold E. Kemp, **PLANNING AND PRODUCING AUDIOVISUAL MATERIALS,** Revised Edition

Arthur E. Ring and William J. Shelley, **LEARNING WITH THE OVERHEAD PROJECTOR**

Robert M. W. Travers, **MAN'S INFORMATION SYSTEM**

PREPARATION OF INEXPENSIVE TEACHING MATERIALS

Second Edition

Text and Illustrations by

JOHN E. MORLAN

California State University,
San José

CHANDLER PUBLISHING COMPANY

An Intext Publisher

New York   London

Contents

Preface

A common goal of teachers everywhere is to make lessons vital, alive, and lasting for their students. Whether preparing for a presentation, developing a lesson for use in a learning center, or working with students in small groups, teachers find that locally produced instructional media of all kinds lend meaning, depth, and variety to the learning situation.

As teachers use this manual they should consider student involvement in preparing materials. Teachers or students may prepare and use these materials to summarize, interpret, and communicate with others.

The contents of this manual are geared for teachers who have had little or no technical background in materials preparation. Teachers and older students will find that many of the processes may be accomplished without special materials or equipment, and all can be completed with little expense in relation to the usefulness of the finished product. Each chapter and each process within that chapter may be treated separately as an independent unit. When alternatives are available for preparing materials an approach requiring no special equipment and utilizing readily available materials is presented first, followed by more complex procedures that require special equipment. Thus, teachers and students may prepare many of the materials they need at home, or—if they wish—may use special equipment to do a more professional job at school or in an instructional-materials center.

In addition to procedures usually included in a university course in instructional-materials preparation, many new and unique classroom-tested ideas are included here. Teachers on all grade levels and in all subject areas will find something in this book that will be useful to them. However, in a book of this length it is impossible to include an exhaustive coverage of procedures for instructional-materials preparation. Teacher ingenuity and student creativity will greatly expand the application of ideas presented here.

I am greatly indebted to colleagues and students who have shared with me their ideas and suggestions concerning this book. Professors Hailer, Cochern, and Espinosa of California State University, San José all have given many useful comments and suggestions. Doctors Ray Davidson of Texas Tech, Bob Wagner of Ohio State University, John Dome of Miami University, Wes Meierhenry of the University of Nebraska, and many others have made suggestions through the years which have influenced this work. Karen Hoffman, Marvin Harmon, and many other students have given encouragement and suggestions of importance. My wife Gwen provided invaluable assistance in typing and editing the manuscript. It is to her, and to teachers like her, that this book is dedicated.

John E. Morlan

Materials
for
Projection

I

When they can see a good illustration, students may understand better what a teacher is trying to tell them. This chapter is designed to help teachers and others to supply their needs for projection materials that will help them be more effective teachers. When materials for projection are needed but not available, teachers can prepare their own transparencies and opaque-projection materials by following the suggestions discussed and illustrated in this chapter. Procedures requiring dark-room facilities and special photographic equipment and training, such as the preparation of filmstrips, $2'' \times 2''$ slides, and high-contrast photography, are not included here.

TRANSPARENCIES FOR OVERHEAD PROJECTORS

The overhead projector is in growing use by teachers on all instructional levels, from primary grades to university graduate courses and in virtually all subject areas. Since the projector is versatile, a wide variety of materials can be used in overhead projection to present information visually and vividly with concomitant success in learning for the students. All teachers should know how to use an overhead projector.

Many types of transparencies for overhead projectors can be easily prepared by a teacher who has no previous technical training. More than a dozen of these types are discussed in the pages that follow and their preparation is explained and illustrated. The production of transparency mounts, masking techniques for use with transparencies, and the use of adhesive acetate for the addition of color are also discussed and illustrated.

HAND-DRAWN TRANSPARENCIES

Hand-drawn transparencies may be easily prepared with readily available and inexpensive materials. The drawing may be done on clear, treated, or frosted plastic, usually cellulose acetate. Transparencies are produced in much the same way whether on clear, treated, or frosted material, except that a wider variety of materials and tools may be used with the frosted plastic. Treated acetate is preferred because it absorbs inks more readily than untreated acetate. Reprocessed x-ray film works well and is inexpensive.

HAND-DRAWN TRANSPARENCIES

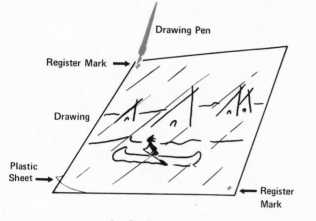

1. Outlining

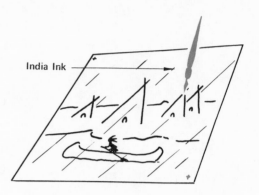

2. Coloring

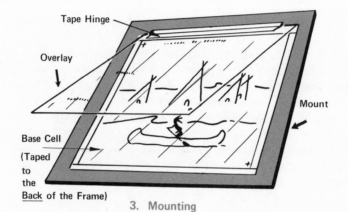

3. Mounting

Materials and Equipment

> engineering tracing paper
> drawing ink; and, if color is important, India inks, slide inks, plastic inks,
>   or felt pens containing various colors of ink
> sharp soft lead (graphite) pencil
> drawing pen and ruler with raised edge
> cardboard mounts (for overlay assemblies)
> pressure-sensitive tape
> acetate (plastic sheets—clear, treated, or frosted, in dimensions appro-
>   priate to the projector size)
> clear plastic spray

Procedure for Clear and Treated Acetate

Prepare the basic detailed drawing in pencil on a sheet of tracing paper or drawing paper, to fit the projector size. Place register marks in the upper left and lower right corners of the pencil drawing. Then:

1. Trace the base-cell outline directly onto the acetate sheet with drawing ink suitable for drawing on plastic.[1] Add register marks and lay the acetate aside to dry.

---

[1] Use *only* inks suitable for drawing on plastic. The additional cost is minimal and well worth the additional investment. Pelikan and Koh-i-noor inks are exceptionally fine.

2. After the ink outline is completely dry, apply color within the desired areas. For each overlay, follow the production procedure outlined for making the base cell.

3. If the transparency is complete on one sheet only, the drawing may be protected from damage by covering it with a second sheet of plastic before taping it to the back of the frame (mount).

An overlay assembly should be mounted either on commercially produced precut frames (mounts) or on cardboard mounts made by the teacher. Attach the base cell to the cardboard mount with pressure-sensitive tape. Mount successive overlays by hinging the plastic film on one edge only with tape, carefully matching the register marks on the overlays and the base cell. Cut the tape so that it does not extend beyond the edge of the film on either side. After all the overlays have been mounted, the transparency assembly is ready for projection.

Procedure for Frosted Acetate

One may follow the same procedure in preparing frosted-acetate transparencies, except that other drawing media may be used, and the finished transparency must be sprayed with clear plastic spray if the projected image is to appear bright on the screen. In addition to India inks suitable for plastics, plastic inks, felt pens, soft lead (graphite) pencils, and slide crayons may also be used.

Drawing should be done on the *dull* side of the plastic.

Coat the completed transparency with a thin coating of plastic spray applied to the frosted surface *except* when felt pens have been used for color. Spraying the frosted plastic will make it more transparent and protect the drawing from damage during use. If felt-tipped pens are used, protect the surface of the transparency with a sheet of clear plastic, for plastic spray on felt-tipped pen inks will often cause them to smear and ruin the transparency.

Take care to follow the manufacturer's directions when applying the coating of plastic spray to avoid smearing or bubbling of the transparency. Do *not* use frosted plastic for overlays.

Materials Sources

Frosted Acetate: Slidecraft Co., Meadows A.V.C. Service.
Prepared Acetate: H. T. Herbert Co.
Prefixed Acetate: Arthur Brown & Bro., Inc.
Clear Acetate:
    Arthur Brown & Bro., Inc.
    Lewis Artist Supply Co.
    Transilwrap Co.
Acetate Inks: Arthur Brown & Bro., Inc.
Reprocessed X-Ray Film: Johnson Plastics, Inc. (E-Z-I Film).

SILHOUETTE PROJECTION

Leaves, arrow points, and other objects may be projected in silhouette. Paper cut-outs may be used to dramatize a story, and paper geometric shapes may be used in mathematics lessons. A piece of yarn and groups of objects in silhouette may be used in developing concepts of set theory.

An additional technique of interest is showing a magnetic field as it occurs around the poles of a horseshoe magnet. To illustrate magnetic field, follow the directions given on the next page.

SILHOUETTE PROJECTION

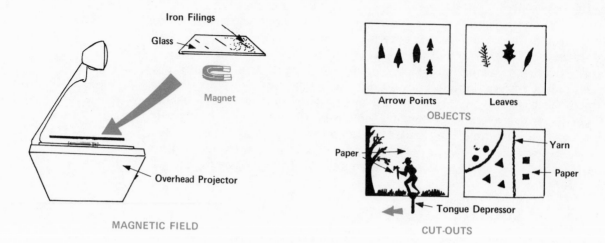

MAGNETIC FIELD

OBJECTS

CUT-OUTS

Materials and Equipment

> magnet
> iron filings
> sheet of glass or plastic
> overhead projector

Procedure

1. Place the magnet on the projector stage.
2. Place the glass or plastic on top of the magnet.
3. Sprinkle iron filings on the glass. The filings will form a magnetic pattern projected for all to see.

ASTRONOMY PUNCH-OUT PROJECTUALS

"How can I help my students develop more interest in astronomy?" "What would be a better way to teach such things as constellation forms?" These are questions science teachers often ask themselves, and these questions need to be answered. A way to use the overhead projector to project constellation forms easily and inexpensively is presented in the accompanying illustrations and discussion.

Materials and Equipment

> star chart (encyclopedia is a good reference)
> tracing paper
> pencil
> ruler
> nail or saddle punch
> lightweight cardboard (manila folder)

Procedure

1. Draw a grid on the cardboard with lines 1 inch apart.
2. Draw a grid on a sheet of tracing paper with lines one-half inch apart. Clip the grid on top of the star chart.
3. Use the grid marks on the two grids as reference points and transfer the star pattern to the grid on the cardboard.

4. With a saddle punch or nail, punch out holes where you wish stars to appear in projection. If a nail is used to make holes in the cardboard, be sure to use sandpaper to remove the raised cardboard around the holes, so that the holes will not close in projection. Your constellation projectual is now ready to use.

Place the cardboard sheet on the overhead projector. Focus the light points on the screen and dim the room lights. The constellation will appear dramatically in white against a darkened screen.

You can also project the constellation onto the chalkboard, then with chalk mark the place of each star. This is a quick, easy, and accurate way to transfer the illustration from the cardboard to the chalkboard.

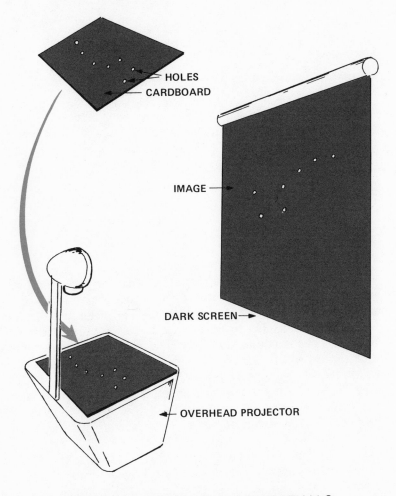

HOLES

CARDBOARD

IMAGE

DARK SCREEN

OVERHEAD PROJECTOR

ASTRONOMY PUNCH-OUT PROJECTUALS

SPIRIT-DUPLICATOR ("ditto") TRANSPARENCIES

Teachers may use the spirit duplicator to produce color transparencies suitable for projection. This process is especially useful for preparation of transparencies to go with duplicated materials that are to be handed to the class. However, the material projected on the screen will *not* be as bright as that in a hand-drawn transparency.

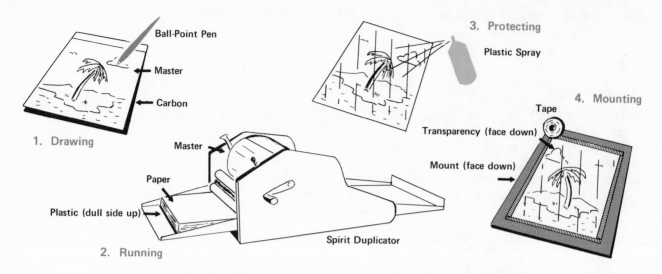

1. Drawing — Ball-Point Pen, Master, Carbon

2. Running — Master, Paper, Plastic (dull side up), Spirit Duplicator

3. Protecting — Plastic Spray

4. Mounting — Tape, Transparency (face down), Mount (face down)

Materials and Equipment

spirit duplicator
frosted-acetate sheet
duplication carbon master(s)
drawing instrument(s)
duplicator paper
plastic spray
cardboard mount
pressure-sensitive tape

Procedure

Assemble the needed materials. Then:

1. Prepare the master as would be done for paper-duplicated copies. For lettering, a primary typewriter, or any one of a number of lettering instruments, can be used. A ball-point pen or hard lead pencil can be used for the preparation of any needed drawings. For each color desired on the finished "dittoed" paper copies and accompanying transparency, insert a separate color carbon sheet, carbon side *up*, beneath the master, before drawing the section that is to appear in color.

2. Place the frosted acetate sheet, *dull side up*, under the stack of paper to be run through the machine. Feed the paper, then the frosted acetate, through the duplicator. *Hand feed the acetate* into the machine to insure successful printing.

3. Place the printed acetate *dull side up* on a sheet of paper and coat evenly with plastic spray. Be sure to follow carefully the spraying directions printed on the can, to avoid getting an uneven finish on the surface of the transparency. Allow to dry for at least two minutes, or until the surface is hardened.

4. Mount the completed transparency on a cardboard mount with pressure-sensitive tape. A sheet of clear acetate may be placed on top of the spray-coated side of the transparency, and mounted simultaneously with it, to further protect the printed surface.

Materials Source

Frosted Acetate: Arthur Brown & Bro., Inc.

THERMAL-COPY OR HEAT-TRANSFER TRANSPARENCIES (THERMO-FAX)

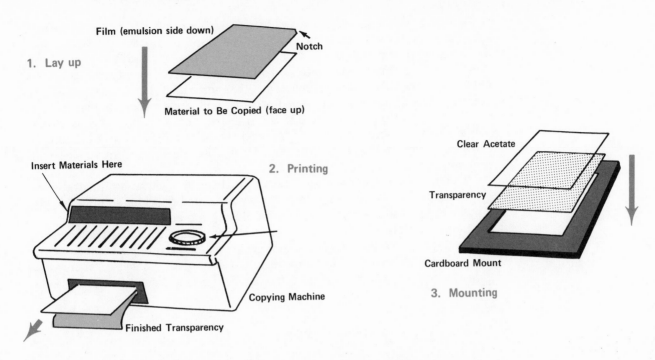

1. Lay up

Film (emulsion side down)

Notch

Material to Be Copied (face up)

2. Printing

Insert Materials Here

Copying Machine

Finished Transparency

3. Mounting

Clear Acetate

Transparency

Cardboard Mount

THERMAL COPY OR HEAT-TRANSFER TRANSPARENCIES (THERMO-FAX)

Newspaper reports, magazine articles, charts, graphs, pictures, and most typed, written, or drawn materials may be produced in transparency form for projection, employing Themo-Fax copying machines and transparency films. No photographic developing solutions are necessary. People inexperienced in audiovisual production can make transparencies by the Thermo-Fax method in a lighted room. Black-line and color-line films are available, as well as other "specialized" films.

When selecting material to copy, or preparing an original, be sure the copy is no *larger in dimensions* than $7\frac{1}{2}'' \times 9\frac{1}{2}''$, although it may be on an $8\frac{1}{2}'' \times 11''$ sheet of paper. Prepare hand-drawn materials in pencil (#1, #2, or IBM), or better yet with a black drawing ink, on *opaque* paper (ledger paper or "ditto" paper rather than tracing paper). Lettering should be large enough to be easily read when projected. For example, primary-typewriter type reads well in projection, while pica and elite types do *not* read well.

Materials and Equipment

> original material to be copied
> Thermo-Fax copying machine
> Thermo-Fax transparency film (positive, negative, and five colors of film are available)
> clear acetate or plastic, size of transparency film
> cardboard mount
> pressure-sensitive tape

Procedure

Arrange the materials on a table so that all are easily within reach. Then:
1. Place the original material to be copied face up on the table, and put a sheet of Thermo-Fax film *face* (emulsion side) *down* on top of the material

to be copied. Place the notch of the film at the upper right-hand corner as illustrated.

2. Set the dial to the appropriate setting for originals drawn or printed with black ink (the setting should be the same as for white paper). For drawings in pencil, move the dial about $1/2''$ from the "white" toward the "buff" setting. Insert the material to be copied together with the transparency film into the copying machine. In approximately four seconds, the completed transparency and copied material will come from the machine.

3. It is usually best to mount the transparency, for Thermo-Fax film is of very light weight, and can be handled better if mounted in a substantial cardboard mount. Place the film on the mount and tape it into place with pressure-sensitive tape.

The transparency may be covered with clear acetate as illustrated to protect it from damage, especially if a grease pencil or water-soluble felt pen may be used to add further information during projection.

Several colors of film may be used in combination in one transparency by overlaying several separately printed sheets. Material to be copied may be easily edited by blanking out unwanted sections with a sheet of plain white paper before placing the copy and film in the Thermo-Fax copy machine.

Materials Source

Thermo-Fax Products: 3M Company.

PLASTIC-BAG TRANSPARENCIES

Common clear-plastic bags, such as Baggies or Glad Bags, may be used to prepare transparencies if minute details are not needed. At very little expense students may prepare transparencies for use in social-studies projects or for projection of student creative-writing examples. Heavier-weight plastic sleeves[2] are even better than light-weight bags. These bags currently are available at a cost of about 3 for 10¢.

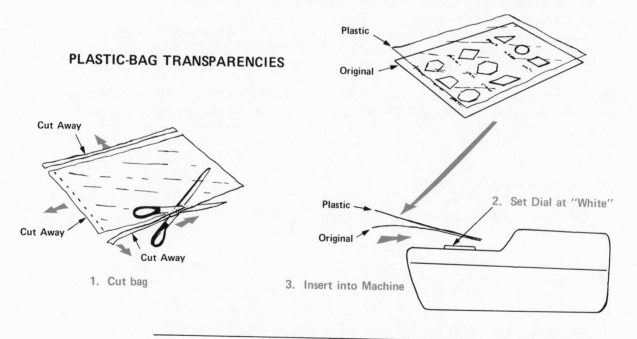

PLASTIC-BAG TRANSPARENCIES

1. Cut bag

2. Set Dial at "White"

3. Insert into Machine

---

[2] Plastic sleeves are available from Dorfman Products, 23813 Archwood Street, Canoga Park, California 91304.

original, drawn or printed in black (for details, see the preceding project, Thermal-Copy or Heat-Transfer Transparencies)
thermal copy machine
plastic bag

Procedure

1. Cut the bottom and sides of the bag off (as illustrated).
2. Set the dial on the copy machine for white paper.
3. Place one piece of plastic on the original and insert, plastic *up*, into the machine. After printing, tape to the back of a frame with masking tape, if desired. *Note*: The white image will appear *black* on the screen.

DIAZO (AMMONIA-PROCESS) TRANSPARENCIES

The professional quality and permanence of ammonia-process (diazo) transparencies make them very popular with teachers. To produce these transparencies requires certain very special materials, and teachers interested in making ammonia-process transparencies should arrange with the school audiovisual director for a supply.

Three different kinds of equipment for transparency printing are described here. For directions in using others, see the manufacturer's suggestions which accompany the machine to be used.

Materials and Equipment

engineering tracing paper
pens, ruler and other instruments for drawing or tracing
India ink
1-one-gallon jar with screw top, or commercial developing unit
sponge, to be placed in the bottom of the jar
masking tape, or other pressure-sensitive tape
diazo (ammonia-process) film (size according to the projector available);
    several colors of film are available
transparency printer, or printing frame
cardboard mounts (for overlay assemblies)
soft lead (graphite) pencil
concentrated ammonia or household ammonia

Procedure for Producing an Overlay Assembly Using a Beseler Printer or a Printing Frame

The procedure for making a simple one-sheet transparency and the procedure for making a base cell for an overlay transparency are the same. Additional steps are necessary for a production of an overlay assembly.

Arrange the materials to be used on a flat surface. Then:

1. Outline the complete, detailed drawing in pencil on a sheet of plain white paper, making the drawing within a $7\frac{1}{2}'' \times 9''$ area. The finished pencil drawing will serve as the guide for successive drawings to be made on engineering tracing paper with India ink. Place two register marks on the pencil drawings as illustrated.
2. Trace the outline of the base cell from the pencil drawing onto the tracing-paper masters in register to check alignment of all the elements in the proposed transparency assembly.

Choose a color film (usually black) for the base cell (or first plastic sheet in the assembly). Transparency film can be handled in a normally lighted

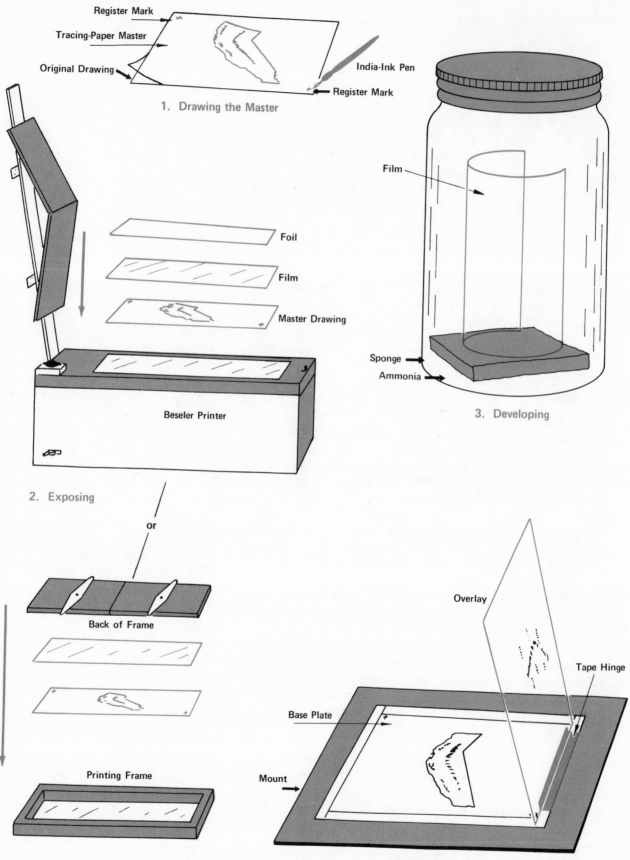

Register Mark

Tracing-Paper Master

Original Drawing

India-Ink Pen

Register Mark

1. Drawing the Master

Foil

Film

Master Drawing

Beseler Printer

2. Exposing

Film

Sponge

Ammonia

3. Developing

or

Back of Frame

Printing Frame

Overlay

Tape Hinge

Base Plate

Mount

4. Mounting

room without fear of light damage. Place the first tracing *face up* in the transparency printer; then place the plastic transparency film *face* (emulsion side) *down* on top of the tracing-paper master with the notch in the upper left-hand corner, cover with a foil (reflective) sheet, and fasten the cover of the transparency printer in place. Set the timer of the printer according to instructions printed on the film box (usually about $2 \frac{1}{2}$ minutes).

If a printing frame is used instead of a transparency printer, place the tracing in it first, then the film, and close the frame. Expose the frame in direct sunlight according to directions of the film manufacturer concerning time and light intensity (which depends upon time of day, time of year, and other factors).

Repeat step 2 for the production of each plastic-film overlay in the assembly, choosing contrasting colors of film for easy identification of separate elements.

3. Place a sponge in the bottom of the jar, pour in about $\frac{1}{4}$ cup of ammonia, and screw the lid into place. Remove the exposed plastic film from the printer, open the jar and drop the film into it; then quickly screw the lid tightly into place. Allow the film to develop in the ammonia fumes until the lines are as dark as desired; then remove the developed transparency film from the jar.

4. Attach the base cell to a cardboard mount with pressure-sensitive tape. When overlays are to be used, it may be convenient to attach the cell plate to the back of the mount. If commercially prepared mounts are not available, mounts can be made by following the directions given in this manual in the section entitled "Transparency Mounts" (page 24).

Mount successive overlays by hinging the plastic film at one edge only with tape, matching register marks on all elements of the assembly carefully as each element is mounted. Cut the tape so that it does not extend beyond the edge of the film on either side. After all overlays have been mounted, the transparency assembly is ready for projection.

Procedure Using Other Diazo Units

Several types of units are in use for exposure and development of diazo films. Some of them have the light stage *above* the slot or tray for insertion

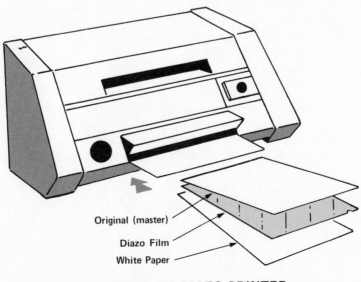

Original (master)

Diazo Film

White Paper

NEWER TYPE OF DIAZO PRINTER

of materials. In such cases, materials are stacked in *reverse order* from that one would use in exposing film in a Beseler printer.

First, prepare the original (tracing-paper master), following the directions given in the discussion for making an overlay assembly using a Beseler printer (page 9). Next, select a film color, and assemble as follows: white paper, film on *top* with notch in *upper right-hand corner*, and master *face down* on *top* of the film. Turn on the machine, set the timer as suggested by the manufacturer, and insert the film into the machine. When the film has been ejected place it in a developing unit until the colors are as dark as desired. Mount on a cardboard frame.

Problems in Diazo Printing and Development

Occasionally teachers have difficulties with diazo printing. If directions are followed but lines appear too light on the film, either the film has been exposed *too long* in the diazo printer (passed too slowly through the machine), the developing unit needs recharging with ammonia, or the film has *not* been left long enough in the developing unit. If the film looks "cloudy" (with color splotches), the film has *not* been exposed long enough. Adjustments in exposure and developing will result in good transparencies.

Materials Sources (Film)

Ansco.
Charles Beseler Co.
Eastman Kodak Co.
Ozalid Division, General Aniline and Film.
Tecnifax Corp.

DIAZO SILHOUETTE TRANSPARENCIES

Leaves, opaque silhouettes of other objects may be cut-outs, and are easily printed on Diazo film if they are opaque, relatively flat, and small. It is *not* necessary to have special printing or developing equipment to obtain good results.

Materials and Equipment

diazo film
overhead projector or printer (for exposure of film)
1-gallon jar with screw top, or commercial developing unit
concentrated or household ammonia
leaves or other shapes to be printed
newspapers
a sheet of white paper ("ditto" paper will do)

Procedure

1. If leaves are to be printed in silhouette, be sure they are dry-pressed and flat. Dry them between folded newspapers with books added as weights on *top* of the papers.

2. Place the leaves or other objects to be printed in silhouette on top of the overhead projector platen (glass). Select a sheet of diazo film, place it on top of the material to be printed, and cover it with a sheet of white paper. Cover the white paper sheet with a stack of folded newspapers, and place books on top to hold the newspapers in place. Turn the overhead projector on, and expose for approximately *five times* as long as you would on a commercial printer. Exposure times may be worked out by using "test

DIAZO SILHOUETTE TRANSPARENCIES

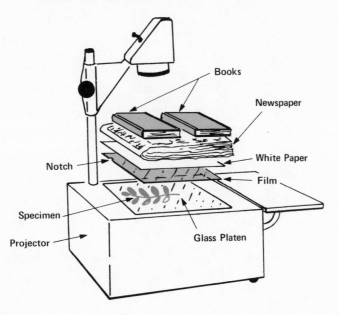

strips" exposed for various lengths of time on the overhead projector to determine appropriate time for exposure. Or use a commercial light box as directed.

3. Remove the film from the overhead projector or from the light box, and place in the developing jar. Be sure the jar has been appropriately charged with ammonia.

4. When the color is as dark as desired, remove the film from the jar. Mount the film on a cardboard frame.

MASTERFAX: TRANSPARENCIES, COPIES, SPIRIT MASTERS

The Masterfax machine will print transparencies, duplicating-paper copies, and preparing thermal masters. One may also laminate materials using this machine, although this operation is not discussed here.

Materials and Equipment (for transparency)

Masterfax machine
material to be copied
heat or thermal-copy film

Procedure

1. Prepare original as you would for any thermal-copy transparency. Materials written, printed, or drawn in carbon will work well (page 7).

2. Place the film *face up* on the glass plate. Note the position of the notch on the film.

3. Place the original *face down* on top of the film.

4. Set the dial to 1 (*average* setting). Turn on the machine, close the lid.

5. Remove from the machine when the light goes off.

Paper copies and spirit masters are made in a similar fashion with settings and arrangements of materials as illustrated.

Materials Source

Ditto (Masterfax Products), Bell & Howell, Inc.

MASTERFAX: TRANSPARENCIES, COPIES, SPIRIT MASTER

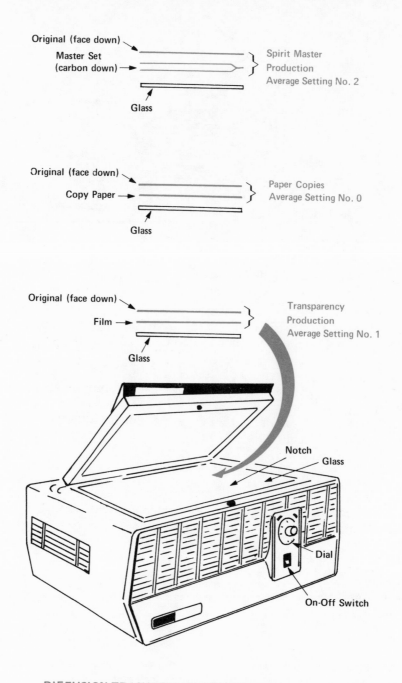

Original (face down)
Master Set (carbon down)
Glass

Spirit Master Production
Average Setting No. 2

Original (face down)
Copy Paper
Glass

Paper Copies
Average Setting No. 0

Original (face down)
Film
Glass

Transparency Production
Average Setting No. 1

Notch
Glass
Dial
On-Off Switch

DIFFUSION-TRANSFER TRANSPARENCIES

Transparencies can be prepared on a combination printer and developer that will copy materials onto a transparent base directly from books or magazines, from typed material, or from work done with ball-point pen, fountain pen, colored pencils and crayons, and spirit duplicators. The Copease machine, discussed here, is one of several makes that can be used to copy from books. The head of the Copease exposure unit is adjustable to any book thickness, and the sponge-rubber pad on the lid of the unit assures uniform pressure and contact of the original material with the negative being printed, facilitating a high quality of reproduction.

book copier (Copease or other)
transparency paper and film—negative and positive for each copy (Copease or other)
original (book, magazine, or other printed material)
developing solutions
cardboard mount
pressure-sensitive tape
scissors
sink with water faucet

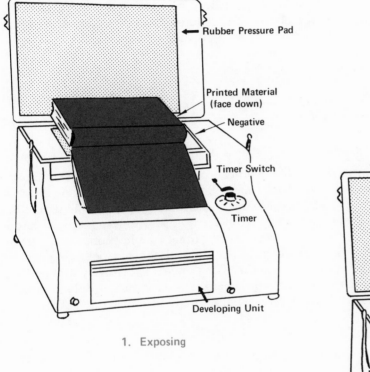

1. Exposing

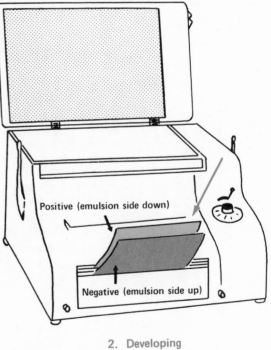

2. Developing

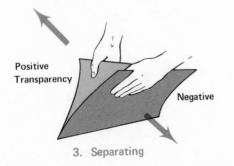

3. Separating

DIFFUSION-TRANSFER TRANSPARENCIES

1. Open the Copease printer (exposure unit) lid, place a sheet of negative film *emulsion side up* on the glass plate, and place the material to be copied *face down* on the film. Adjust the lid of the printer so uniform pressure is exerted on the book, magazine, or other material to be copied, and lock the lid in place.

2. Set the timer according to directions accompanying the machine and film used (usually around 10 to 15 seconds). Push the timer switch to begin the film exposure. After the timer has stopped running, remove the negative from the exposure unit and place the negative and a sheet of positive film one on each side of any bar of the developing unit. Film sheets will be ejected automatically, bonded together.

3. Wait about ten seconds, then separate the positive and negative films. Wash the transparency for about ten minutes in cool water. Mount the positive print on a cardboard mount with pressure-sensitive tape.

Materials Sources

Copease Co.
Transferon: Ozalid Division, General Aniline and Film.
Verifax: Eastman Kodak Co.

HEAT-LIFT TRANSPARENCIES MADE WITH A DRY-MOUNT PRESS

Full-color transparencies for overhead projection may be made inexpensively using a heat-sensitive plastic and a dry-mount press. Magazine illustrations printed on clay-coated paper may be transferred to a durable plastic by following the procedure outlined below. Most illustrations in pictorial magazines such as *Life*, *Holiday*, and many other publications lend themselves to this method. Lightweight laminating plastic has been selected as illustrative of material appropriate for lifting since it is relatively inexpensive and does not require some of the equipment needed to successfully complete the transparencies through the use of more expensive heavyweight plastics.

Materials and Equipment Needed

picture or print to be transferred (see Procedure, Step 1, for requirements).
dry-mount press with temperature control which allows for a setting of 270° Fahrenheit
heat-sensitive film (such as Sealamin—available from Seal, Inc.)
pan or sink full of water
wetting agent, such as household detergent
sheet of cardboard or masonite
scissors
clear plastic (acrylic) spray
protective paper (wrapping or butcher type)
soft cloth
newspaper
old magazine
tacking iron

Procedure

Arrange all the needed materials on a flat working surface. Then:

1. Select pictures to be lifted (transferred). Pictures suitable for lifting must be printed on clay-coated paper. Check to see if the picture you wish

to lift is printed on clay-coated paper by moistening a finger tip and rubbing it gently over the margin surrounding the print. A milky or gray liquid residue should be deposited on your finger tip if the paper is clay-coated. Each picture to be lifted should receive the wet-finger test since some pages in the same issue of a magazine may not be clay-coated. After selecting and testing each picture, remove it from the magazine by cutting out the *entire page*. Do *not* trim the picture at this point.

2. Prepare the dry-mount press by setting the thermostat to 270°F. Proper temperature and extreme pressure are necessary for the production of a good-quality transparency. To gain additional pressure, place a piece of masonite or heavyweight cardboard in the press on top of the rubber pad. Close the press to trap the heat so that the press will heat up more rapidly.

To remove any moisture from the picture, place it in the press under a piece of clean paper for about ten seconds. Remove it from the press, and place on a flat, clean surface.

3. Cut the laminating plastic *slightly smaller* than the page from which the picture is to be lifted. The plastic should extend beyond the picture area

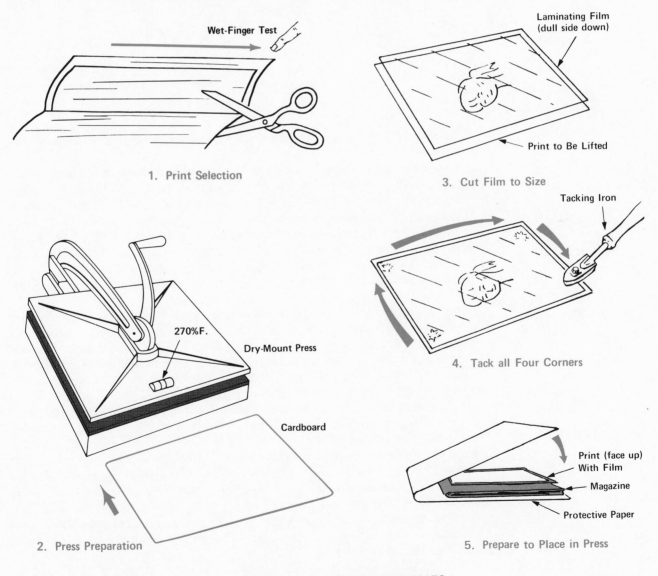

1. Print Selection

3. Cut Film to Size

Laminating Film (dull side down)

Print to Be Lifted

270%F.

Dry-Mount Press

Cardboard

2. Press Preparation

Tacking Iron

4. Tack all Four Corners

Print (face up) With Film

Magazine

Protective Paper

5. Prepare to Place in Press

HEAT-LIFT TRANSPARENCIES

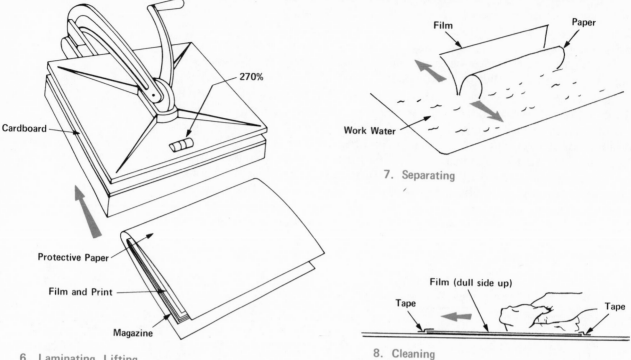

270%

Cardboard

Protective Paper

Film and Print

Magazine

6. Laminating, Lifting

Film   Paper

Work Water

7. Separating

Film (dull side up)

Tape   Tape

8. Cleaning

if possible. Place the *dull* (heat-sensitive) side *down* on the untrimmed picture page.

4. Turn the tacking iron up to "high" setting. Tack the plastic to the picture at all four corners by touching the tip of the iron to the plastic. Heat from the iron will melt the adhesive on the underside of the plastic, causing it to stick to the paper as it cools.

5. Place the print with plastic attached *face up* on top of a large magazine. Take a piece of wrapping or butcher paper, cut it, and fold it around the print and magazine as illustrated. This will protect the plastic surface from any foreign matter which may be on the metal of the heated surface of the press.

6. Insert the pack into the press as illustrated. Close the press, and allow the material to remain in the press for about 30 seconds. Open the press, and remove. Do *not* try to keep the material from curling. It will curl up into a tube shape as it cools. After it cools, look at the material to see if there are any "gray" areas where the plastic may not have adhered to the picture. If necessary, reheat to remove bubbles or gray spots.

7. Place the bonded material in a pan of water and add a little detergent. Soon the paper will begin to pull loose from the plastic. The paper may be completely separated from the plastic after the material has soaked in water for a few minutes. Test to see if the paper is ready to separate by trying one corner. The paper should separate from the plastic quite readily. The inks from the printed material have now been transferred to the laminating plastic. Carefully wipe off clay and paper fibers with a soft, wet cloth. Blot off any excess moisture and allow to dry. Be sure no gray residue (clay) remains on the dull side of the plastic, as clay is opaque and will project *black* on the screen.

8. After the material is completely dry, lay it, *dull side up*, on a sheet of newspaper. Tape the corners to the sheet, taking care *not* to cover any of the

plastic area you wish to project when the transparency is finished. Spray the transparency with several thin coats of plastic spray, allowing each coat to dry before applying successive coatings. Cut and trim the plastic so that it fits over the opening of a transparency frame or mount. Mask off any unwanted material by taping a piece of paper over the portion you do not wish to project. The transparency material should then be taped to a frame, and is thus completed and ready for use.

Materials Source

Seal, Inc.

THERMO-FAX COLOR-LIFT TRANSPARENCIES

By using the Thermo-Fax Color-Lift method, full-color pictures may be transferred to a plastic sheet for projection. Teachers working in schools where heat copy machines (such as Thermo-Fax) are used for doing letter copies can use this method for producing their own full-color transparencies.

Materials and Equipment

Thermo-Fax Copying Machine (or other heat copying machine)
Thermo-Fax Color-Lift Film, and Color-Lift Carrier
picture printed on clay-coated paper (from magazines such as *Holiday*,
   Life, and *National Geographic*)
detergent
pan of water
soft cloth
plastic spray, or Thermo-Fax Color-Lift Brightener and applicator
masking tape, or other pressure-sensitive tape
cardboard mount

Procedure

Assemble all needed materials and place on a clean, flat working surface. Plug in the copying machine and set the dial at the *darkest* setting. Moisten a finger tip and rub it gently over the border surrounding the picture to be lifted. If a gray residue is picked up, the picture is printed on clay-coated paper, as desired, and is suitable for lifting. Remove the picture from the magazine and place *face up* on the table. Then:

1. Cut a sheet of Thermo-Fax Color-Lift Film to the size of the picture to be lifted, and place dull side *down* on top of the picture. Hold the film and picture together, *turn them both over*, and insert into the carrier as illustrated; then, insert the carrier into the Thermo-Fax machine.

2. Remove the bonded original print and plastic film from the carrier and place into a container of water to which has been added some detergent. Allow to soak for two minutes, or until the paper will peel easily from the plastic. Remove the material from the water and peel the paper from the film beginning at one corner. If the paper will not pull loose easily, allow to soak for a while longer; then complete the separating process.

3. Place the transparency dull side *up* on a flat surface. Using a soft wet cloth, gently remove the clay residue and paper fibers from the plastic. Hang to dry.

4. After the plastic is dry, place on a flat surface and spray the dull side with clear plastic spray, or apply Color-Lift Brightener. Allow to dry thoroughly.

5. When the spray has dried, tape the transparency to a cardboard mount with pressure-sensitive tape.

THERMO-FAX COLOR-LIFT TRANSPARENCIES

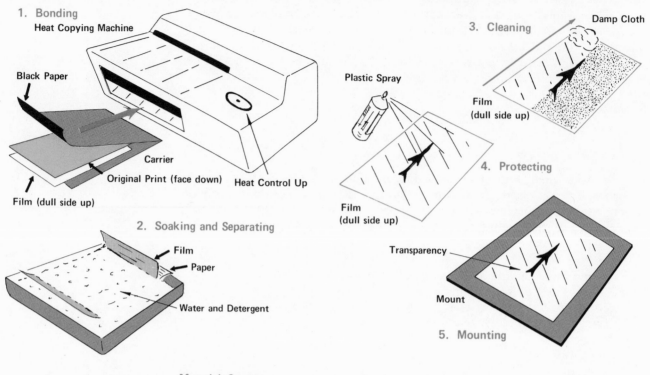

1. Bonding

Heat Copying Machine

Black Paper

Carrier

Original Print (face down)   Heat Control Up

Film (dull side up)

2. Soaking and Separating

Film

Paper

Water and Detergent

3. Cleaning

Damp Cloth

Plastic Spray

Film (dull side up)

4. Protecting

Film (dull side up)

Transparency

Mount

5. Mounting

Materials Source

Thermo-Fax Products: 3M Company.

LIFT TRANSPARENCIES MADE WITH ADHESIVE TRANSPARENT SHELF PAPER

For those unable to conveniently use a dry-mount press and heat-lamination film in the preparation of lift transparencies, adhesive transparent shelf paper[3] may be used as an alternate material. Pictures printed on clay-coated paper may be successfully lifted from the page through the steps outlined below.

1. Determine if the illustration is printed on a clay-coated paper by rubbing a moistened finger along the edge of the page beside the picture to be lifted. If a gray residue comes off on your finger, cut out the entire illustration from the magazine, and place *face up* on a clean, smooth surface. Cut the shelf paper *larger* than the picture to be lifted, peel back the protective covering at one corner, and adhere the transparent material to the table and picture as illustrated. Allow the plastic and the covering sheet to curl over, as illustrated, as you work.

2. Move a ruler diagonally down across the picture, smoothing out any bubbles which may occur as you go. Hold the ruler at an angle as illustrated. Continue until the entire page area is covered.

3. Trim off excess shelf paper, up to the edge of the magazine page. *Rub out any gray spots or bubbles with a spoon or the back of a comb.*

---

[3] Widely available under the trade name "Con-Tact" and also under other brand names. Although universally called shelf paper, the material is a plastic film carried on a protective paper backing. It is this plastic film that is used to make the transparency; the paper backing is discarded.

4. Soak the bonded material in warm water to which a little hand soap or detergent has been added.

5. When the paper begins to soak loose from the plastic, gently peel the paper off. The inks have now been transferred to the plastic adhesive surface of the shelf paper.

6. Clean off clay and paper fibers by gently rubbing with a soft, damp cloth. Allow to dry. If there is still some gray residue (clay) on the plastic, reclean with a damp cloth until all residue has been removed. Allow to dry. Spray the sticky, dull surface with a plastic spray, and allow to dry. Use

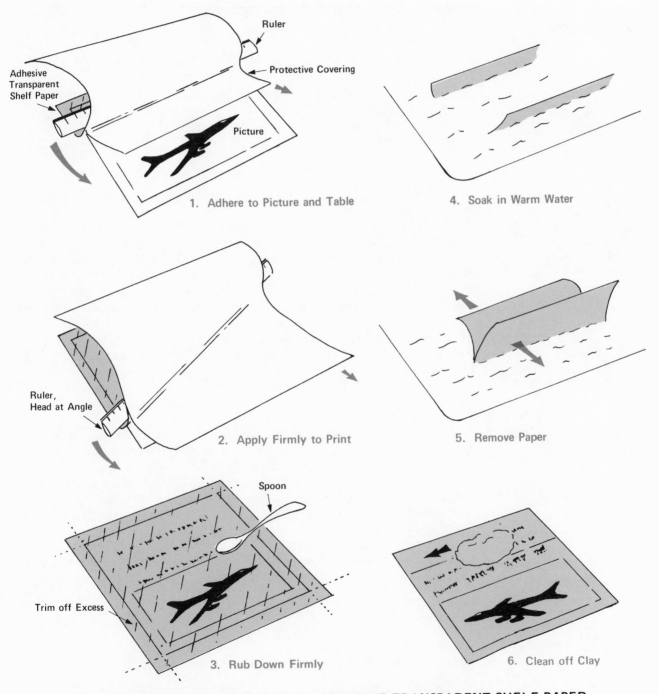

1. Adhere to Picture and Table

4. Soak in Warm Water

2. Apply Firmly to Print

5. Remove Paper

3. Rub Down Firmly

6. Clean off Clay

LIFT TRANSPARENCIES MADE WITH ADHESIVE TRANSPARENT SHELF PAPER

several coats of spray to insure good coverage, to make the transparency more durable, and to cover the sticky side of the plastic with a hard, non-adhesive protective film. The transparency is now ready to trim and attach to a transparency mount with pressure-sensitive tape.

CHEMICAL-BOND LIFT TRANSPARENCIES

Plastic lamination film which works on the chemical-bond principle may be used in producing full-color lift-process transparencies without special equipment. Film such as Plain-Vu may be used by beginners to lift prints from clay-coated paper with excellent results.

Materials and Equipment

> picture or print to be transferred (see Procedure, step 1, for requirements)
> two sheets of chemical-bond laminating plastic film
> pan of water
> wetting agent, such as household detergent
> 6" ruler or comb

Procedure

Secure all needed materials and arrange them on a clean, flat working surface. Then:

1. Select prints to be lifted (transferred). Pictures to be lifted must be printed on clay-coated paper if an acceptable transfer is to be accomplished. Check to see if the picture is printed on clay-coated paper by wetting a finger tip and rubbing it gently over the border surrounding the print to be lifted. A milky or gray liquid residue should be left on the finger tip if the print is on clay-coated paper. Each picture should receive the wet-finger test, since some pages in the same issue of a magazine may be clay-coated while others may not. After selecting and testing each picture, cut it from the magazine and it is ready for lifting. Cut the plastic film to size and remove the protective backing sheet from the adhesive side of the film.

2. Place the print face *up* on the working surface, and carefully position the film, adhesive side *down*, on the face of the print. Rub with a 6" ruler or a comb to insure complete adhesion.

3. Place the bonded materials in a pan of water, and add about a teaspoon of household detergent. Allow to soak for about 30 minutes.

4. Remove the bonded materials from the water, and gently pull the paper from the plastic. The printed material will have been transferred to the plastic, and at this point the plastic film is translucent. Carefully wipe off clay and paper fibers with a soft, wet cloth. Blot off any excess moisture and allow the film to dry.

5. When the film is completely dry, cover the unprotected surface with another sheet of plastic film to complete the transparency. It will be ready to project as soon as this bond has taken place.

Materials Source

Plain-Vu Film: The Carr Corp.

ADHESIVE ACETATE

Adhesive acetate is convenient to use for the addition of color tones, symbols, or patterns. It is available in sheets or rolls.

CHEMICAL BOND LIFT TRANSPARENCIES

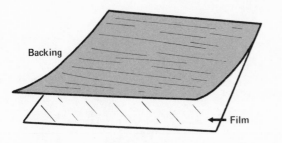

Backing

Film

1. Removing Backing

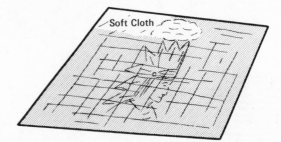

Film

Print

2. Bonding Print and Film

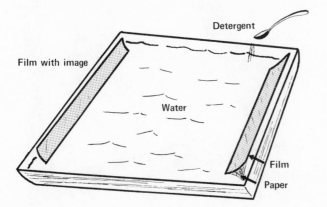

Detergent

Film with image

Water

Film

Paper

3. Paper and Film Separation

Soft Cloth

4. Cleaning

Plastic Film

Transparency

5. Finishing

adhesive acetate of the desired color or pattern
basic transparency, complete except for color addition
stencil knife or razor blade
scissors

Procedure

Complete the transparency except for the color. Then:

1. Use scissors to cut a section of adhesive acetate slightly larger than the area to be covered.

2. Peel off the protective backing sheet.

3. Press the adhesive acetate into place on the base transparency, working out all air bubbles and wrinkles. Carefully cut off all excess acetate with

ADHESIVE ACETATE

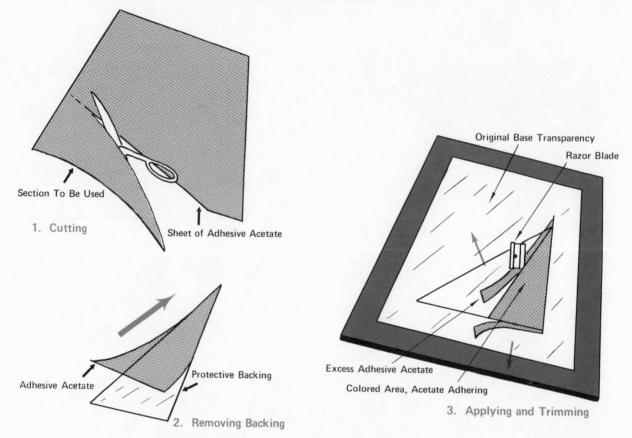

Section To Be Used

1. Cutting

Sheet of Adhesive Acetate

Adhesive Acetate

Protective Backing

2. Removing Backing

Original Base Transparency

Razor Blade

Excess Adhesive Acetate

Colored Area, Acetate Adhering

3. Applying and Trimming

a razor blade, using the outline of the area to be colored on the base transparency as a guide. After peeling off the excess acetate, rub the edges of the colored acetate firmly into place. The transparency is now ready to project. (*Note*: Adhesive acetate is especially useful in preparing graphs for projection. Cut the adhesive acetate into strips, remove the backing, and apply the strips directly to the surface of the transparency materials.)

Materials Sources

Add-A-Color Sheets: Arthur Brown & Bro., Inc.
Add-A-Tint Shading Sheets: Arthur Brown & Bro., Inc.
Colotone Overlay Sheets: Bourges, Inc.
Contack Shading Sheets, Color Tints: Transograph Co.
Presto-Tone Shading Sheets, Presto Color: Arthur Brown & Bro., Inc.
Zip-A-Tone Screens, Zip-A-Tone Colors: Para-Tone, Inc.
Artype Screens: Artype, Inc.

TRANSPARENCY MOUNTS

Acceptable cardboard mounts for overhead-projection transparencies may be easily made if commercial mounts are not available.

Materials and Equipment

eight-ply cardboard (or poster board)   pencil
razor blade or knife   scissors or trimming board
ruler, metal or metal-edged

With scissors or a trimming board, cut the cardboard to size $12'' \times 10''$. Outline the area to be cut out on the cardboard, using the appropriate illustration as a guide. Place the ruler along the lines drawn on the cardboard, and *carefully* cut out the desired area with a razor blade. Use caution to avoid slashing fingers. Make a *shallow* cut first. Repeat cutting with *medium* pressure until the cut is completely through the board.

TRANSPARENCY MOUNTS

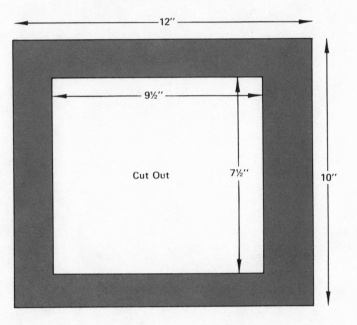

TRANSPARENCY-MASKING TECHNIQUES

Progressive disclosure of items on transparencies for overhead projectors is often advantageous when viewers are to be led through a discussion together, step-by-step. A transparency which might be confusing if revealed all at once may be made clear and useful when portions are successively revealed and fully discussed. One base transparency may serve to present several steps in a sequence, instead of a series of separate transparencies.

The base transparency should be fastened to a cardboard mount with pressure-sensitive tape. Masking strips should be cut from light cardboard or from opaque plastic. Hinges for the masking strips may be made from strips of pressure-sensitive tape, or commercially prepared hinges may be used. Strips of pressure-sensitive tape can also be used to cover captions or labels, and removed during the presentation as discussion progresses. Tape may also be placed over captions and labels when the transparency is to be used in testing situations. All tape hinges and tape cover-up strips are shown in *red* on the accompanying illustrations.

Several examples of successful masking techniques for different purposes are presented on the following pages. Select and use the technique which best meets a specific communication need.

Materials Source

Hinges and Opaque Plastic: Tecnifax Corp.

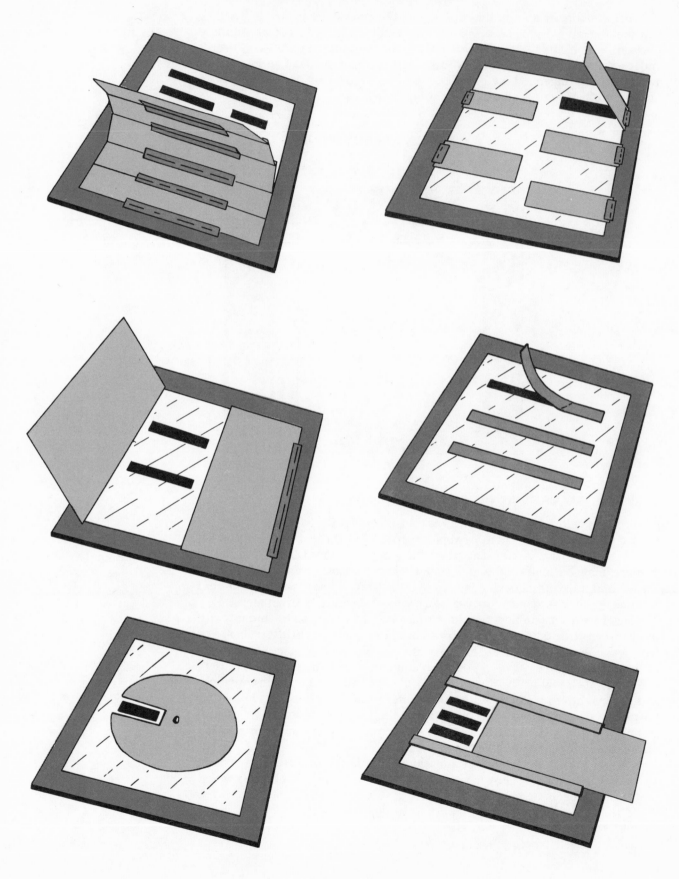

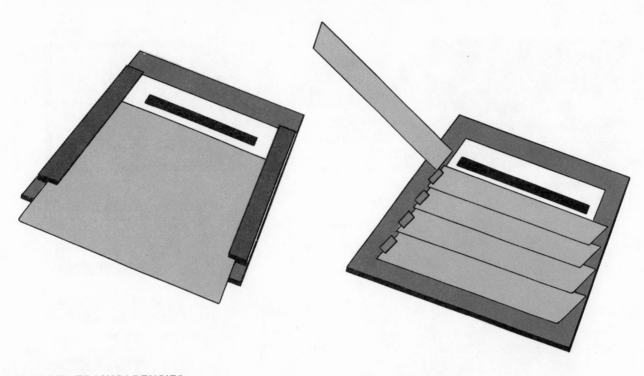

POLAROID TRANSPARENCIES

Polaroid slides may be easily produced by inexperienced photographers, and are excellent projection materials for use with reports, lectures, and demonstrations. Special Polaroid transparency film and mounts are supplied to make either the $3^{1}/_{4}'' \times 4''$ or $2^{1}/_{2}'' \times 2^{1}/_{2}''$ slides. The $2^{1}/_{2}'' \times 2^{1}/_{2}''$ slide can be easily trimmed for use as a $2'' \times 2''$ slide, if allowance is made for trimming when the picture is taken. Maps, charts, nature-study photos, highlights of field trips, and dramatic presentations can all be effectively captured for projection on transparent film.

Materials and Equipment

Polaroid camera
Polaroid transparency film, type 46-6
hardening solution
dip tank
lifting tool
$3^{1}/_{4}'' \times 4''$ Polaroid plastic mounts, or $3^{1}/_{4}'' \times 4''$ glass
binding tape
copy stand for copy lenses (if needed)

Procedure

Purchase the necessary film and other materials. Select the subject for photographic reproduction. Get the subject in focus and trip the shutter. Pull the tab to begin the developing process. Then:

1. Tear off the tab as illustrated.

2. Allow the film to develop for two minutes. Open the back of the camera and remove the transparency from the camera along the perforated lines by using a special metal lifting tool, as illustrated. Be careful *not* to touch the film emulsion while handling the transparency.

POLAROID TRANSPARENCIES

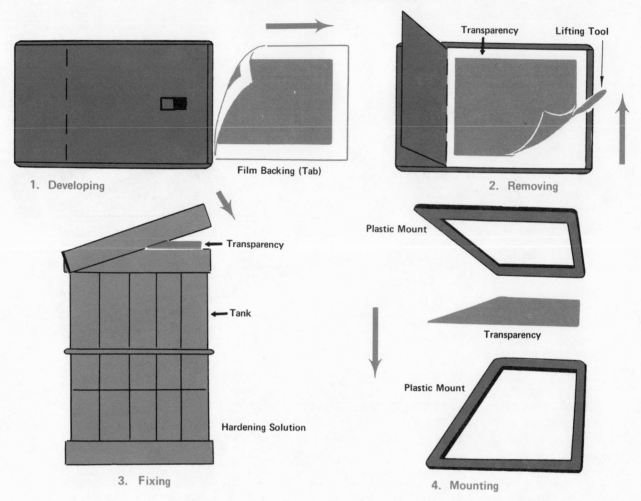

1. Developing

Film Backing (Tab)

Transparency   Lifting Tool

2. Removing

Transparency

Tank

Hardening Solution

3. Fixing

Plastic Mount

Transparency

Plastic Mount

4. Mounting

3. Immerse the film in hardening solution in the tank for at least ten seconds.

4. Remove the transparency from the tank with a smooth, even pull to prevent damaging the film with the lips of the dipping tank. Mount the transparency in the appropriate mount.

If copy work is to be done from a magazine, book, or photograph, it is advisable to use a copy stand and copy lenses. Each shot will produce a single transparency $3\frac{1}{4}'' \times 4''$, or $2\frac{1}{2}'' \times 2\frac{1}{2}''$ according to the film used. In copying material for use as $2'' \times 2''$ slides, four or six photographs of the same size can be arranged on the copy stand, copied on one $3\frac{1}{4}'' \times 4''$ piece of transparency film, developed, hardened, and then cut into four or six smaller sizes suitable for use as $2'' \times 2''$ slides.

To use $3\frac{1}{4}'' \times 4''$ Polaroid transparencies on an overhead projector, first cut a piece of cardboard large enough to cover the glass platen. Then cut a rectangle opening in the cardboard a *little less* than $3\frac{1}{4}'' \times 4''$. Place this cardboard mask on the projector. Move the projector *away* from the screen until light fills the projection area. Place the Polaroid transparency on the opening to project.

Materials Source

Transparency Film: Polaroid Corp.

OPAQUE PROJECTION MATERIALS

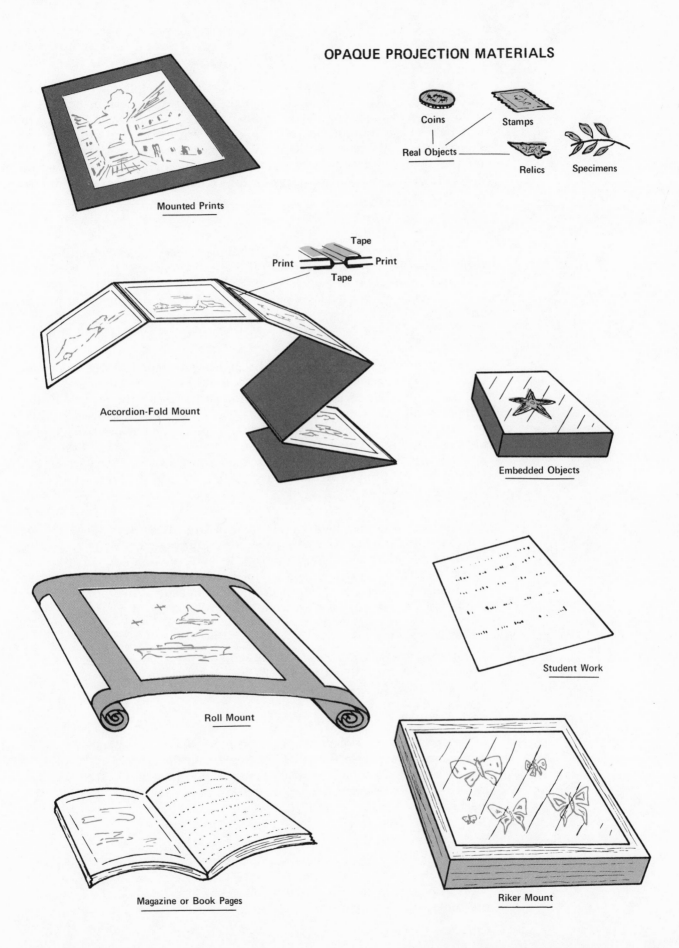

Mounted Prints

Coins   Stamps

Real Objects   Relics   Specimens

Tape   Tape

Print   Print

Accordion-Fold Mount

Embedded Objects

Roll Mount

Student Work

Magazine or Book Pages

Riker Mount

OPAQUE PROJECTION MATERIALS

The opaque projector provides a means for projecting mounted prints, student work, magazine or book materials, small real objects, materials embedded in plastic, and specimens mounted in Riker mounts. Various types of materials suited for opaque projection and suggestions for utilization of these materials are presented here. (*Note*: Since opaque projectors typically focus a relatively great amount of heat on objects being projected, take care not to leave materials in the projector for prolonged periods of time, as heat damage may result.)

MOUNTED PRINTS

Prints mounted by any of the techniques presented in "Mounting Pictorial Materials" can be projected in the opaque projector. For ease of handling, prints should not be larger than 8″ × 10″. If the opaque projector has a roll attachment, prints may be rolled in one side and out the other quickly and easily.

Accordion Fold

Mounted prints may be fastened together with tape to form sets easily used in opaque projection. To construct accordion-fold sets, line the prints up side by side *face down* on a clean, flat surface, with the *bottom* of the prints toward you, allowing a space of ⅛″ between prints. Hinge the prints together with pressure-sensitive tape; then turn the line of prints over, *face up*. Apply strips of tape to the *top* side of the assembly to fasten the edges of the prints together. Fold the prints together and place information on the back of the first print to facilitate easy identification of the print set.

Roll

Prints or drawings may be ironed to a strip of Chartex (page 43), or permanently mounted on heavy paper strips for presentation in roll form. When positioning materials on the roll, be sure to allow enough space between illustrations so only one complete illustration will be projected at one time. Write identifying information on the outside of the roll. The rolled prints curl and need a glass plate to hold them flat in the projector.

STUDENT WORK

Student work may be presented unmounted for analysis or criticism. It is suggested that the student's name be covered or folded under before presenting material for the class to see.

MAGAZINE OR BOOK PAGES

Magazine or book materials may be presented in the opaque projector without removing them from the binding. To facilitate focusing, a sheet of heat-resistant glass should be placed over bound materials before they are inserted into the opaque projector, unless a sheet of glass is built into the machine.

REAL OBJECTS

Real objects such as coins, stamps, small relics, and botanical specimens may be placed in the projector for presentation. A contrasting background sheet of paper or cardboard should be used to help bring out the details of such objects more clearly.

Objects embedded in plastic should be fastened to card stock before being projected, to help insure against dropping and breaking the object. A loop of transparent tape may be used to hold the embedded material to the card stock.

Riker Mount

Riker-mounted specimens can be used in the opaque projector without any special physical preparations. (See page 52 for instructions on preparing a Riker mounting.)

WORK SHEETS TO ACCOMPANY PROJECTED MATERIALS

Learning achieved with projected materials is often enhanced and made more lasting if the individual student is given "handouts" or work sheets to be used in connection with the projected materials.

Spirit-duplicated materials are easily prepared for such purposes, and two methods of making spirit-duplicator masters are discussed here: multicolor spirit masters and thermal spirit masters.

MULTICOLOR SPIRIT ("DITTO") MASTER

Spirit ("ditto") masters may be prepared which will duplicate paper materials in two or more colors with *one pass* of the paper through the machine. Colors may be used for emphasis of important points and to break down a complex presentation into components for analysis and for ease of understanding.

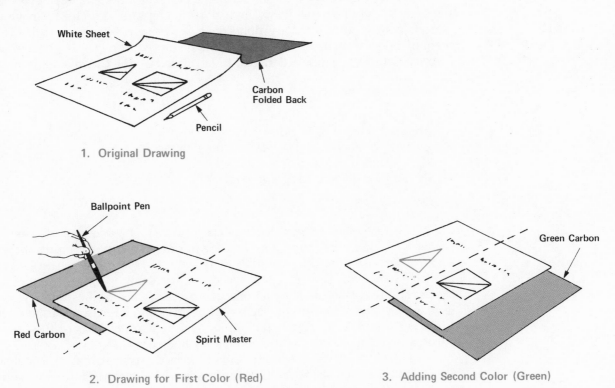

White Sheet

Carbon Folded Back

Pencil

1. Original Drawing

Ballpoint Pen

Green Carbon

Red Carbon

Spirit Master

2. Drawing for First Color (Red)

3. Adding Second Color (Green)

MULTICOLOR SPIRIT ("DITTO") MASTER

two or more colors of spirit masters, as needed (illustration shows red and green)
pencil
ball-point pen
spirit duplicator
duplicator paper
original drawing or material to be duplicated

Procedure

1. Draw or trace the entire drawing in pencil on the white-paper side of the master unit, carbon folded back and away, as illustrated.

2. Fold the carbon back under, and draw with ball-point pen or type only what you wish to have in the basic color (red in the illustration). Tear off the carbon and place to one side.

3. Slide the second-color carbon underneath the master and add the second color by drawing only over the pencil lines you wish to appear in the second color on the duplicated material as illustrated (green in the illustration).

4. Complete the master by adding the other colors as in step 3. The spirit master is then ready to run.

Materials Source

Ditto, Inc., Bell and Howell.

THERMAL SPIRIT MASTERS

Material printed, typed, or drawn using carbon- or metallic-base inks may be used to produce excellent thermal spirit masters. Articles from newspapers or magazines, or copy done on a typewriter will work well. Use a medium-inked ribbon, and a backing sheet *behind* your paper, if a typewriter is to be used in preparing an original to be copied by the thermal method.

Materials and Equipment

thermal copy machine
original material to be copied
packing sheets (several sheets of "ditto" paper)
thermal spirit masters
carrier (if required with your master)

Procedure

1. Two types of thermal masters are available. One requires the use of a carrier while the other type does not. If your master carbon requires the use of a carrier, assemble the materials as follows: (a) Place the packing sheets ("ditto" paper) on the table, (b) place the original *face up* on the packing sheets, and (c) place the thermal master on the original as illustrated. If you have a master *not* requiring a carrier, place the thermal master on the table, tissue up. Insert the original face up *under* the carbon. Discard the brown paper which comes with the thermal master before proceeding.

2. If you must use a carrier, place it with the transparent or silk sheet face up on a table. Insert the previously assembled materials, thermal spirit master on top, into the carrier. If you are *not* using a carrier, the materials which are arranged as described in the first step for use *without* a carrier are already arranged properly for insertion into the machine.

THERMAL SPIRIT MASTER

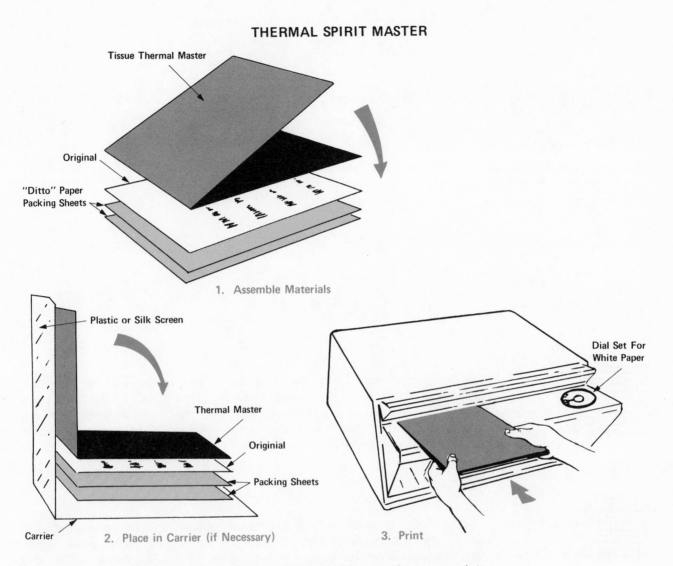

Tissue Thermal Master

Original

"Ditto" Paper
Packing Sheets

1. Assemble Materials

Plastic or Silk Screen

Thermal Master

Originial

Packing Sheets

Carrier

2. Place in Carrier (if Necessary)

Dial Set For
White Paper

3. Print

3. Set the control knob on the copying machine to the appropriate setting (usually the same as the setting for white paper), turn the machine on, and run the loaded carrier through. Open the carrier and remove the thermal master. Peel the carbon sheet from the master slowly and carefully, and discard. The master is now ready to run.

Materials Source

The 3M Company.

Mounting
and
Preserving

II

Teachers are repeatedly confronted with the problem of how to mount and preserve materials for repeated use as instructional tools. Techniques appropriate for mounting pictorial materials and various techniques for mounting specimens such as coins, insects, and botanical materials are discussed and illustrated in this chapter.

MOUNTING PICTORIAL MATERIALS

Excellent methods of mounting materials include permanent and temporary rubber-cement mounting, dry mounting with photographic mounting tissue, adhesive-paper mounting, wet mounting on cloth, and dry mounting on cloth.

RUBBER-CEMENT MOUNTING

Although rubber-cement mounting of materials is more time-consuming than some other methods, it is possible through the use of this technique to achieve professional results with materials readily available in most schools.

Materials and Equipment

item to be mounted, trimmed to final dimensions
trimming device, trimming board, or scissors
rubber cement
brush for spreading cement
pick-up (a piece of tacky rubber to which cement will cling; you can make one by rolling partly dried cement into a small ball)
mounting board, such as poster board or railroad board, cut to size
two sheets of waxed paper, large enough to cover the mounting board completely and overlap
soft lead (graphite) pencil
plastic spray or shellac (a brush is also necessary if shellac is used), or laminating materials and equipment

Arrange the material to be used in the mounting process on a table, easily within reach. Then:

1. Center the print on the mounting board, leaving a margin at the bottom of the print slightly larger than those at the top and sides. With a soft lead pencil, register the placement of the picture on the mounting board, using the corners of the picture as a marking guide.

2. Turn the print over, place it on a newspaper or other work sheet, and apply rubber cement to the back of the print, taking care not to get rubber

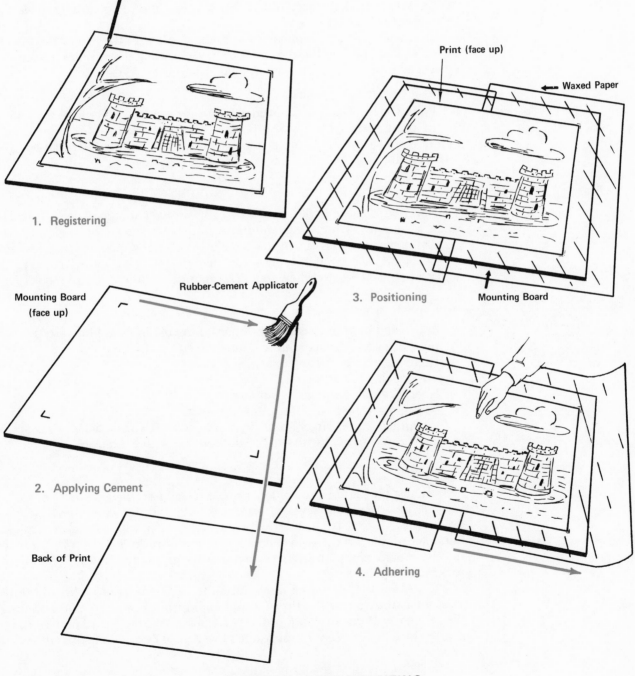

1. Registering

Print (face up)

Waxed Paper

3. Positioning

Mounting Board

Mounting Board
(face up)

Rubber-Cement Applicator

2. Applying Cement

Back of Print

4. Adhering

RUBBER-CEMENT MOUNTING

cement on the picture front, as the rubber cement may dissolve inks used in printing. Apply cement to the face of the mounting board, being sure to cover the area which the picture will occupy after mounting. Any cement on the edges of the mounting board can be easily rubbed off later, after the picture is mounted.

3. When the cement is completely dry (has lost its glossy appearance) cover the mounting board with two sheets of waxed paper, overlapping the paper near the center of the mounting board as illustrated. Position the picture on top of the waxed paper, taking care to align the picture with the register marks on the mounting board.

4. Slide out one of the waxed sheets, smoothing the face of the print as the cement-coated surfaces touch. Go through the same procedure as the other waxed sheet is removed.

Remove any excess cement by rubbing it off with the tips of the fingers or a pick-up. Preserve the mounted print by coating it with plastic spray or clear shellac, or cover with laminating plastic (pp 43-48).

Procedure for Temporary Mounting

Follow steps 1 and 2 as outlined in the procedure for permanent mounting of prints. After coating the back of the print with rubber cement and before the cement dries, place the print on the mounting board and rub it into position.

DRY-MOUNTING WITH PHOTOGRAPHIC MOUNTING TISSUE

Dry-mount tissue is often used by professional photographers and artists when a smooth, wrinkle-free and uniform bond is needed in preparing materials for display. This tissue is available from photographic supply outlets, in sheets or rolls. One may use the material without special training to achieve excellent results when graphics are to be mounted to card stock.

Materials and Equipment

dry-mount press and tacking iron, or household iron (as illustrated)
print or picture to be mounted, untrimmed
trimming device (cutting board or scissors)
card stock, such as railroad board
large sheet of clean paper (butcher paper will do)
books, magazines, or photographic weights
mounting tissue, larger than final dimensions (Kodak tissue, Seal MT-5 and Seal Fotoflat with press; Seal Fotoflat with hand iron)

Procedure

Arrange the material to be used on a table, and set the iron to "wool," or turn on the dry-mount press. If a press is used with MT-5 or Kodak tissue, set to 225°. If Fotoflat is used with the press, set to 180°. To insure against bubbling of the print, remove any excess moisture from it by placing it in the dry-mount press for a few seconds, or by pressing with a hand iron before mounting. Then:

1. Attach the mounting tissue near the center of the back of the print with a tacking iron or the tip of a household iron. Use a sheet of mounting tissue slightly larger than the print. If a household iron is used in mounting, Seal's Fotoflat tissue gives best results. Use Seal MT-5 or Kodak tissue with a press.

2. Trim the picture and mounting tissue simultaneously (to insure that the mounting tissue and print are the same size). You may use a piece of

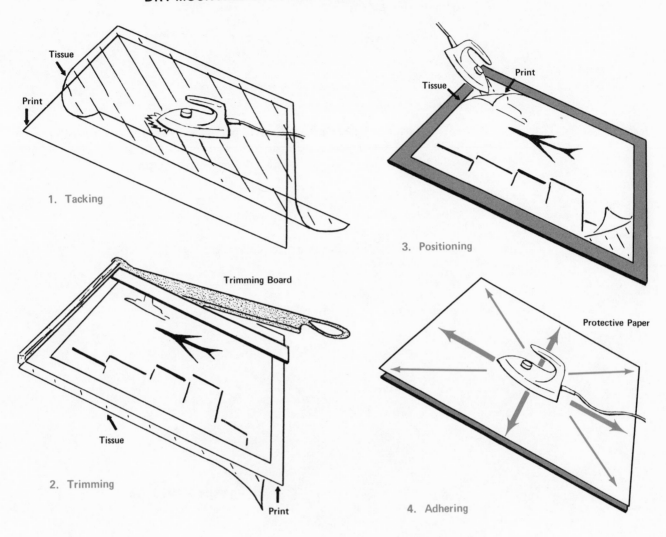

1. Tacking

2. Trimming

3. Positioning

4. Adhering

heavy cardboard or a large ruler held next to the edge of the cutting board (as illustrated) to keep the picture and tissue flat. Otherwise, a crooked cut may result if the paper "humps up" during cutting.

3. Place the pictorial material on the mounting board, allowing approximately the same margin around the print at the sides and top, with a slightly wider margin at the bottom. Attach two opposite corners of the tissue to the board with the tip of an iron.

4. If a household iron is used in mounting the print, be sure it is clean, so foreign matter will not come off the iron onto the face of the print. It is wise to cover the print with a sheet of clean paper before applying heat to the print. Work the iron from the *center* of the picture to the *outer edges*. Move the iron slowly, using a circular motion.

If a dry-mount press is used, place the print and board between the folds of a sheet of protective paper, and insert the pack into the preheated press for at least five seconds. Remove the mounted print from the press.

Place books or photographic weights on top of the print as it cools to prevent buckling of the mounted material.

To protect the mounted print from damage, you may laminate it with transparent adhesive shelf paper or with heat-lamination film, or coat it with plastic spray or shellac. If shellac is used, apply it with smooth, even strokes, moving in the same direction.

Materials Sources (Dry-Mounting Tissue)

Seal, Inc.
Eastman Kodak Co.

ADHESIVE-PAPER MOUNTING

When used as directed, adhesive paper such as Dri-Mount will give a smooth, permanent bond. Adhesive-paper mounting may be accomplished easily and smoothly without the aid of expensive equipment.

Materials and Equipment

    sheet of adhesive paper, size of print to be mounted
    suitable print
    protector sheet (smooth white paper)
    mounting board
    scissors
    6″ ruler or comb
    clear varnish, plastic spray, or laminating plastic

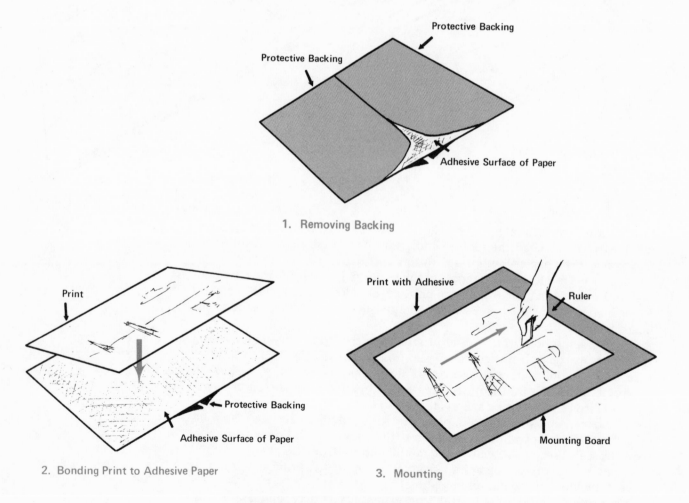

1. Removing Backing

2. Bonding Print to Adhesive Paper

3. Mounting

ADHESIVE-PAPER MOUNTING

Arrange the needed materials on a flat working surface. Then:

1. Cut the adhesive paper to the size of the print to be mounted. Remove the protective backing sheet from one side of the adhesive mounting paper.

2. Press the print to be mounted on the exposed adhesive-coated surface. If any wrinkles form they may be removed by slowly lifting a corner of the print until the wrinkle is reached and pulled out. When the print is smooth and in the position desired, cover it with the protector sheet and rub firmly with a 6″ ruler, or the back of a comb.

3. Remove the remaining protective backing sheet, then place the print lightly on the mounting board. Position as desired and press into place. Again cover it with the protector sheet and rub firmly with the back of a comb or 6″ ruler to create a firm bond.

Protect the surface of the print with clear varnish, plastic spray, or laminating plastic.

Materials Source

Dri-Mount: The Carr Corp.

WET-MOUNTING ON CLOTH

Wet-mounting of materials on cloth requires no special equipment or expensive materials, and helps prolong the life of instructional materials by making them more durable.

Materials and Equipment

map, chart, or print to be mounted
muslin or flour-sack material
wheat paste, such as wallpaper paste
basin or pan of water
pan or bowl for use in mixing the paste
brush or roller for application of the paste
thumb tacks
rolling pin
paper strips (newspaper or butcher paper will do)
smooth waterproof surface that will take thumb tacks (painted press-
    board is a very good surface for this process; frame the edges of the
    pressboard mounting surface with soft wood strips)
soft lead (graphite) pencil
clear plastic spray or shellac

Procedure

Secure all needed materials, and prepare the mounting surface. Then:

1. Coat the surface of the map or print with a thin coat of plastic spray or shellac, and allow it to dry. Then, prepare the paste by pouring a cup of water into the mixing bowl and adding paste *slowly*, mixing, as paste is added, to avoid lumps. Continue to stir the mixture, adding paste or water as necessary, until the paste has a creamy consistency. Soak the cloth in water until it is thoroughly wet. Gently squeeze out any excess water, lay the material on the waterproof surface, and smooth out wrinkles and pockets of air. The threads of the cloth should run parallel with the edges of the waterproof surface. Tack the cloth down at three corners as illustrated. [1. Tacking (1)]

WET-MOUNTING ON CLOTH

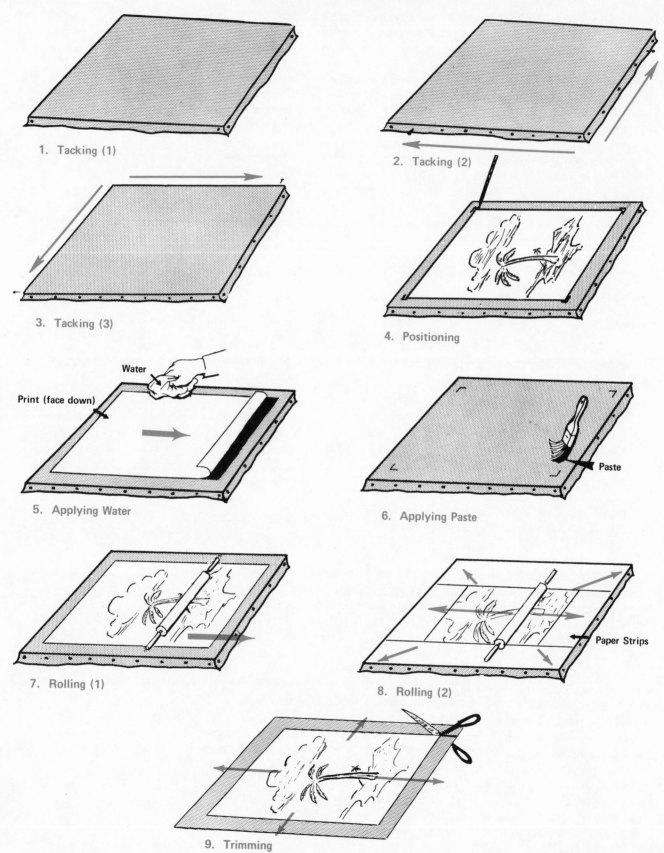

1. Tacking (1)

2. Tacking (2)

3. Tacking (3)

4. Positioning

5. Applying Water

Water
Print (face down)

6. Applying Paste

Paste

7. Rolling (1)

8. Rolling (2)

Paper Strips

9. Trimming

2. Proceed with the tacking process, working from two corners toward the third tack as illustrated. Alternate from one side to the other in tacking. [2. Tacking (2)]

3. Tack down the fourth corner. Fill in the remaining two sides with tacks evenly spaced, working toward the fourth corner from the two sides previously secured. Be sure to eliminate any slack which may occur during the tacking process. [3. Tacking (3)]

4. Place the material to be mounted face up on the muslin, and draw reference marks on the cloth on all four corners with a soft lead pencil.

5. Place the pictorial material *face down* on a clean surface, and apply water to the back of the material until it lies flat and limp on the table.

6. Apply paste to the secured cloth with a brush (or roller) using uniform strokes to obtain a smooth, thin coat of paste. Extend the coated area slightly beyond the reference marks.

7. Place the map into position on the cloth, using the pencil reference marks as a guide. With a rolling pin, roll across the surface of the pictorial material from the *center* to each *side*, then from *center* to each *corner*, as illustrated. Take care *not* to roll over the edges of the pictorial material, as

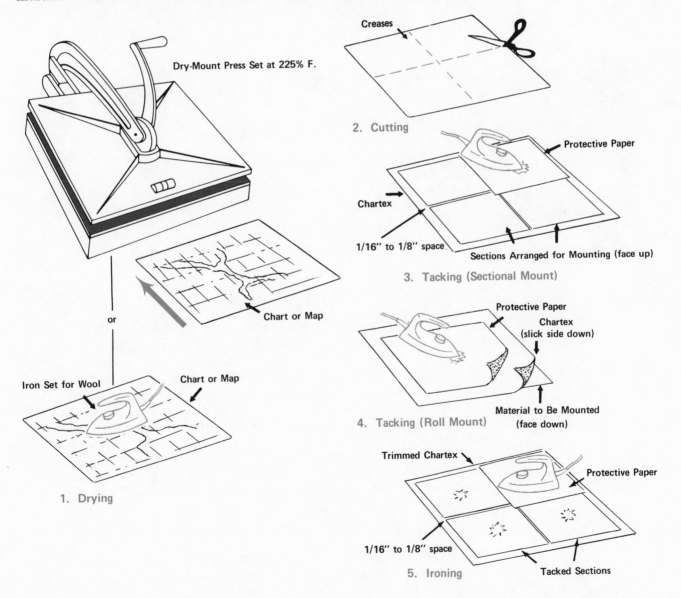

Dry-Mount Press Set at 225% F.

Chart or Map

or

Iron Set for Wool   Chart or Map

1. Drying

Creases

2. Cutting

Protective Paper

Chartex

1/16" to 1/8" space   Sections Arranged for Mounting (face up)

3. Tacking (Sectional Mount)

Protective Paper

Chartex (slick side down)

Material to Be Mounted (face down)

4. Tacking (Roll Mount)

Trimmed Chartex

Protective Paper

1/16" to 1/8" space   Tacked Sections

5. Ironing

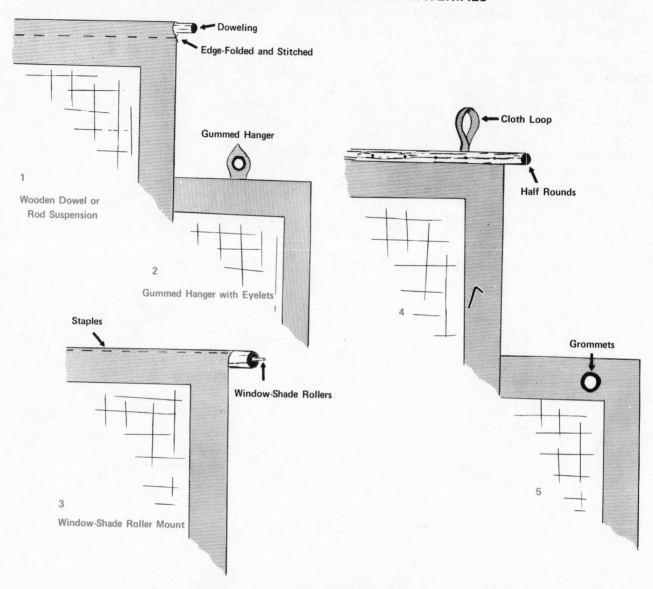

this will result in depositing paste on the surface of the print. Lift corners of the print as necessary to relieve any tension built up during the rolling process.

8. Carefully place paper strips overlapping the edges of the pictorial material and the cloth surface. Roll lightly from the center of the map onto the paper strips. Repeat this process until all four edges of the pictorial material have been secured to the surface of the cloth. Remove and discard the paper strips.

9. Allow the mounted pictorial material to dry completely; then, trim off excess cloth, and finish the project by application of grommets or hangers or by using other techniques described following the discussion of "Dry Mounting on Cloth" (page 43).

DRY-MOUNTING ON CLOTH

Dry mounting of materials on cloth may be quickly and easily accomplished with Chartex, an inexpensive adhesive-impregnated cloth specially prepared for cloth backing of charts, maps, and other pictorial or graphic materials. Chartex is available in sheet or roll form, in widths up to 42″, and lengths of several yards.

Materials and Equipment

> dry-mount press and tacking iron, or hand iron
> Chartex of the desired dimensions (slightly larger than object to be mounted)
> chart or map to be mounted
> several clean sheets of paper
> scissors (it is desirable to have a trimming board as well)
> plastic spray, or shellac and brush
> several heavy books

Procedure

Place all materials needed for dry mounting on a flat, clean surface. Then:

1. Set the dry-mount press on 225° F. (if the press has a temperature-control device) and dry the map by placing it in the press for a few seconds, or set the hand iron at "wool" and iron the map.

2. If the chart or map is large, and it is to be folded for ease of storage, a *sectional mounting* should be considered. To prepare a map or chart for sectional mounting, fold it to the desired storage size; then, open it, lay it on a table, and cut it carefully into sections, using the creases made in folding as guides.

3. If a *sectional mounting* is to be done, lay the sections of the map or chart *face up* on the slick side of a sheet of Chartex, leaving a space of approximately 1/16″ between sections. Tack each section individually to the dry-mount cloth with an iron as illustrated. Be sure to use a protective sheet of paper between the iron and map or chart.

4. If the map or chart is to be *rolled* for storage, place the map or chart face down on a flat surface, and tack a sheet of Chartex, slick side down, to the back of the map or chart. Use a protective sheet of paper between the iron and pictorial material. Simultaneously trim the map and cloth to size.

5. Place the bonded material on a table with the map or chart *face up*, and cover with a clean sheet of paper. Iron with a hand iron or place in the dry-mount press for about five seconds. If a hand iron is used, move slowly with a circular motion, from the center of the section to be mounted to the outer edges. Mount only a section at a time when working with large maps, charts, or prints, and remember always to keep a sheet of paper between the heat applicator and pictorial material.

Place the freshly mounted map or chart on a flat surface, and put heavy weights, such as books, on top of the pictorial or graphic material until it cools. Finish the map or chart by using one of the illustrated suspension techniques.

Materials Source

Chartex: Seal, Inc.

LAMINATING FLAT GRAPHICS

Often teachers prepare materials with great care only to have them soiled or ruined during the first classroom use. To protect prints and other materials from damage caused by handling, dust, or moisture, you may use various laminating techniques to apply a piece of transparent plastic film to the surface of such flat graphic materials as drawings, pictures, or prints.

LAMINATION WITH ADHESIVE TRANSPARENT SHELF PAPER

Adhesive transparent shelf paper (called "paper" although it is a plastic film) is an excellent medium for protecting pictures, small charts, posters, games, flash cards, and other materials which are to be handled by students and used repeatedly or which must last over an extended period of time. This material is a clear plastic, coated on one side with an adhesive which will hold it in place when pressed firmly onto a smooth, clean, dry surface. You may write on the plastic surface with a water-soluble felt-pen ink, and remove what was written with a damp cloth. This feature enables the teacher to use the laminated materials in a wide variety of ways. Adhesive transparent shelf paper may be purchased from almost any large hardware or home-supply store. It is relatively inexpensive and may be applied as a laminating material without the use of special equipment.

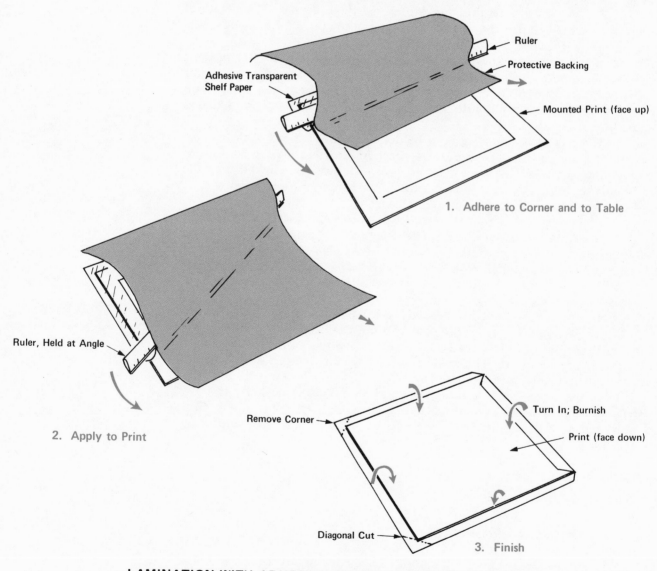

Ruler
Protective Backing
Adhesive Transparent Shelf Paper
Mounted Print (face up)

1. Adhere to Corner and to Table

Ruler, Held at Angle

2. Apply to Print

Remove Corner
Turn In; Burnish
Print (face down)

Diagonal Cut

3. Finish

LAMINATION WITH ADHESIVE TRANSPARENT SHELF PAPER

material to be laminated
clean table
scissors
adhesive transparent shelf paper ("Con-Tact" or other)
small comb
large ruler

Procedure

1. Place the material to be laminated face up on a clean, flat surface, such as a table top. Before removing its protective backing, cut the shelf paper so that it is approximately $1/2''$ wider on all sides than the material to be protected. Remove the protective backing from one corner only by peeling the backing back underneath the plastic (which should be facing you). Adhere the exposed corner of the lining to the table and to a corner of illustrative material.

2. Pull the protective backing from *underneath* the transparent film of shelf paper, following with a ruler *held at an angle* pressed firmly on the surface of the plastic. Allow the unseparated material to curl over on top as illustrated. Check as you go, to see if any bubbles are developing underneath the plastic shelf paper. If so, work the air out by rubbing with a forefinger toward a nearby open area. Move the ruler as you work at an angle across the surface of the plastic shelf paper as illustrated.

3. Pull the plastic shelf paper loose from the table, and turn the print over so that it is *face down* on the table. With a pair of scissors or a knife, cut diagonally across the exposed plastic at the corners as illustrated. Fold the excess plastic against the edges and onto the back of the laminated print. After all four edges have been sealed, turn the print over, and rub down firmly with the back of a comb or short ruler to insure a good bond. The lamination procedure is now completed.

HEAT LAMINATION USING A DRY-MOUNT PRESS

Heat-sensitive laminating plastic applied with a dry-mount press provides a tough, durable protective covering for flat graphics such as drawings or pictures. One brand, Sealamin, may be purchased in rolls of various widths and costs approximately the same as adhesive shelf paper but gives a harder finish after lamination than one gets with transparent plastic shelf paper.

Materials and Equipment

laminating plastic, such as Sealamin
mounted print, drawing, or picture
dry-mount press, set to 270°
tacking iron or hand iron
scissors
old magazine
large books to be used as weights, or photographic weight
sheet of butcher paper or wrapping paper

Procedure

1. If only *one side* of the mounted material needs protection, cut a piece of plastic long enough to lap over onto the back about $1\frac{1}{2}''$ at *both ends*. Lay the print face down on the *dull* side of the laminating plastic. Set the tacking iron to "hi" or the hand iron to "cotton" and tack both ends of the

HEAT LAMINATION USING A DRY-MOUNT PRESS

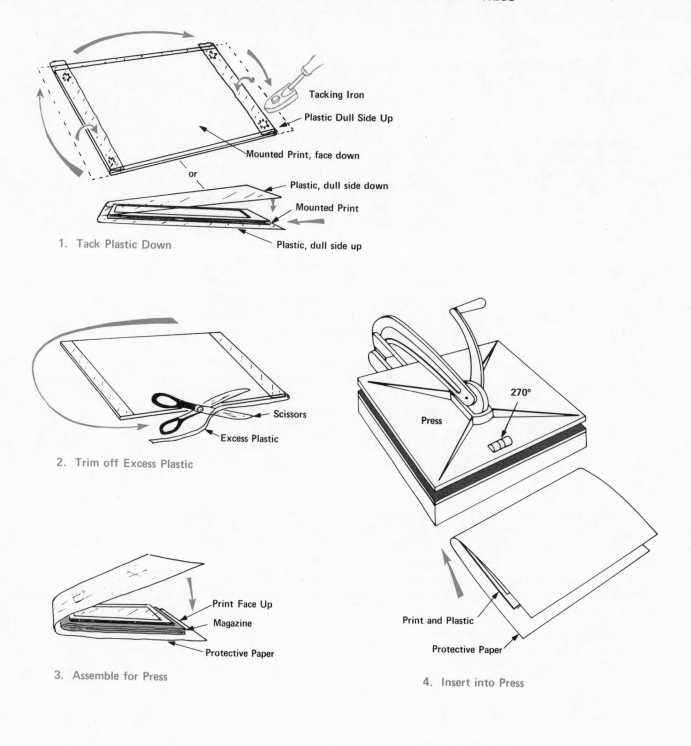

Tacking Iron

Plastic Dull Side Up

Mounted Print, face down

or

Plastic, dull side down

Mounted Print

Plastic, dull side up

1. Tack Plastic Down

Scissors

Excess Plastic

2. Trim off Excess Plastic

270°

Press

Print and Plastic

Protective Paper

Print Face Up

Magazine

Protective Paper

3. Assemble for Press

4. Insert into Press

Books

Laminated Print

5. Cool under Weights

plastic to the mounting stock by touching the iron to the plastic at the corners as illustrated. If the material is to be protected on *both* sides cut a sheet of plastic and lay the print on the *dull* side of the film, fold over, and seal the *two ends* of the plastic together with a tacking iron or hand iron.

2. After tacking or sealing the plastic, trim off the excess plastic on both sides up to the edge of the mounted print.

3. Cut a large piece of paper (butcher paper or brown wrapping paper), place a magazine on top, place the film-covered print on top of the magazine *face up*, and fold the protective paper over as shown.

4. Insert the assembled materials into a press preheated to 270° for 15 to 30 seconds.

5. Remove the laminated material from the press and place *quickly* under a photographic weight or books, as illustrated. Allow to cool for a few seconds before removing weights. The material is now laminated and ready for years of classroom use. If the bond is *not* complete, reheat in the press.

Materials Sources

Glassoloid Corporation of America.
Seal, Inc.

PLASTIC HEAT LAMINATION, THERMO-FAX METHOD

Flat pictures may be laminated quickly, easily, and economically by the Thermo-Fax heat-lamination method, if an office heat-copying machine is available. The resulting plastic covering gives a protective finish that is impervious to damage by dirt or moisture.

Lightweight prints mounted on light card stock can be laminated by this method, but if a heavy backing for prints is desired, the lamination *must* be done *before* mounting.

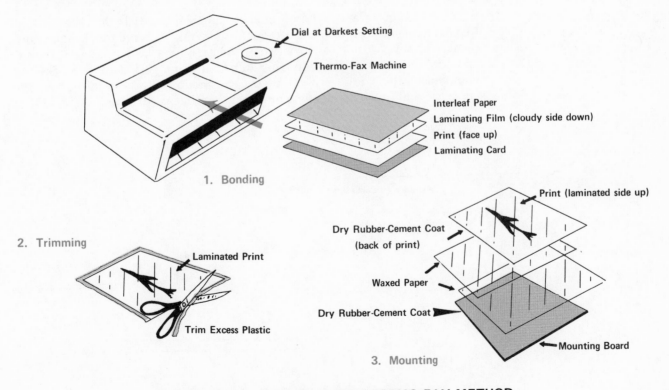

PLASTIC HEAT LAMINATION, THERMO-FAX METHOD

Thermo-Fax laminating film
print to be laminated
laminating card
interleaf paper
scissors

If the print to be mounted on heavy card stock, see the discussion of "Rubber-Cement Mounting" for necessary materials.

Procedure

Assemble all materials and equipment needed and place on a flat working surface. Turn the copying machine on and set the dial to the darkest, or hottest, setting. The print to be laminated should be *slightly smaller* than the laminating film. Then:

1. Place the print *face up* on the laminating card, the laminating film *dull side down* on the print, and the interleaf paper on top of the film; then, insert the materials into the copying machine.

2. After the laminated material comes from the machine, remove from between the interleaf paper and laminating card and trim off excess plastic.

3. Mount the laminated print on card stock by following the directions given in the discussion, "Rubber-Cement Mounting"; or, if both sides of the print are to be laminated, laminate the *other* side by repeating the laminating procedure. *Always laminate only one side at a time.*

Materials Source

Thermo-Fax Film: The 3M Company.

MOUNTING AND PROTECTING SPECIMENS

Often teachers and children collect valuable materials that they would like to share with the group, but because these materials are fragile and easily damaged they are not used, or when they are used they become damaged and are useful for instruction only during a short period of time. Several techniques which are very useful for the mounting of specimens are discussed and illustrated, including mounting specimens with laminating plastic,

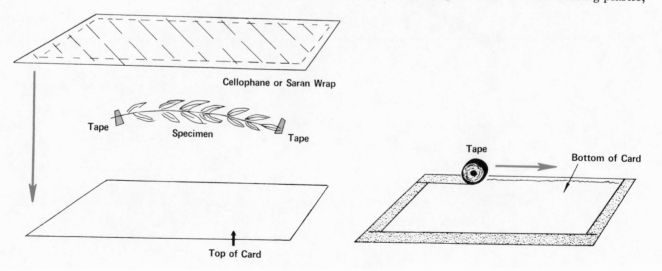

CELLOPHANE MOUNTING

gelatine mounting of specimens, embedding materials in plastic, Riker mounting, match-box mounts, and cellophane mounting on study cards.

Herbarium (plant) specimens may be preserved for use in study and display by mounting on a study card, as illustrated. For more durable protection, use transparent adhesive shelf paper or heat-lamination plastic (pp 43-48).

Procedure

1. Tape the specimen to the top of the study card.
2. Cover the card and specimen with cellophane or Saran wrap, cut to overlap the card edges by ½ ″ or more.
3. Fold the overlapping edges of the cellophane around the edges of the card and tape to the back of the card.

MOUNTING SPECIMENS UNDER ADHESIVE TRANSPARENT SHELF PAPER

Adhesive transparent shelf paper may be used to laminate and preserve previously dried and pressed herbarium specimens or plants, thus protecting them from damage, and retarding deterioration. Although not as durable as heat lamination (pp. 43-48), this technique is far superior to using cellophane or nonadhesive plastic as a covering for specimens taped to card stock—the usual way of preserving collected plant specimens. A discussion of the use of shelf paper to laminate prints or other illustrations is found on page 44-45 . Before beginning the mounting of specimens, read the section in this book devoted to lamination with adhesive transparent shelf paper.

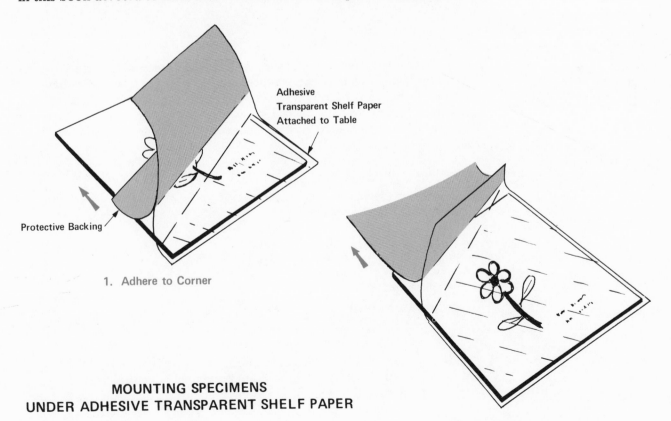

Adhesive
Transparent Shelf Paper
Attached to Table

Protective Backing

1. Adhere to Corner

**MOUNTING SPECIMENS
UNDER ADHESIVE TRANSPARENT SHELF PAPER**

2. Apply to Carded Specimen

card stock
dried specimen
scissors
adhesive transparent shelf paper ("Con-Tact" or other)
small comb or short ruler
large ruler
clean flat surface (such as table)

Procedure

1. Be sure the specimen is pressed flat and is relatively dry. Do *not* try to mount plants until at least a week after they have been collected. Place the plant between pages of a magazine or newspaper, and put several books on top to hold it flat. Let the plant dry. Cut the card stock to the desired size and place it on the table. Position the specimen on the card stock. Be certain it is no closer than 1″ from any edge of the cardboard. Cut the adhesive shelf paper so that it is 2″ longer and 2″ wider than the herbarium card (card stock). Peel the protective covering back at one corner. Stick the exposed plastic to the table top and cardboard allowing 1″ overlap on the top and side as illustrated. Carefully pull the protective covering *out* from *under* the plastic.

2. Apply the plastic shelf paper to the carded specimen, taking particular pains to see that the specimen is caught in place *before* continuing with the lamination process. Some teachers find a ruler helpful in insuring even placement of the plastic while completing the lamination (page 45). Finish the mounting as you would finish a laminated print. Your specimen is now preserved and ready for use.

MOUNTING SPECIMENS WITH HEAT-LAMINATION PLASTIC

Heat-sensitive laminating plastic, such as the plastic manufactured under the trade name Sealamin, is very useful for mounting specimens that lend themselves to flat mounting. Flowers or insects protected by Sealamin will not deteriorate as easily as specimens covered with cellophane, and will last for years of normal classroom use. Sealamin is available in sheet form or in rolls.

Materials and Equipment

laminating plastic, such as Sealamin
mounting board (cardboard)
dry-mount press
trimming board or scissors
large books for weighting purposes
old magazines
dried specimen
tacking iron or hand iron

Procedure

Preheat the press by setting the thermostat to 270°. Close the press and turn it on. When the desired temperature is reached open the press.

Be sure the plant specimen is dry. If you suspect moisture may still be present place the specimen between folds of a paper towel and press between pages of a magazine. Place the magazine into the preheated press for a few

MOUNTING SPECIMENS WITH HEAT-LAMINATION PLASTIC

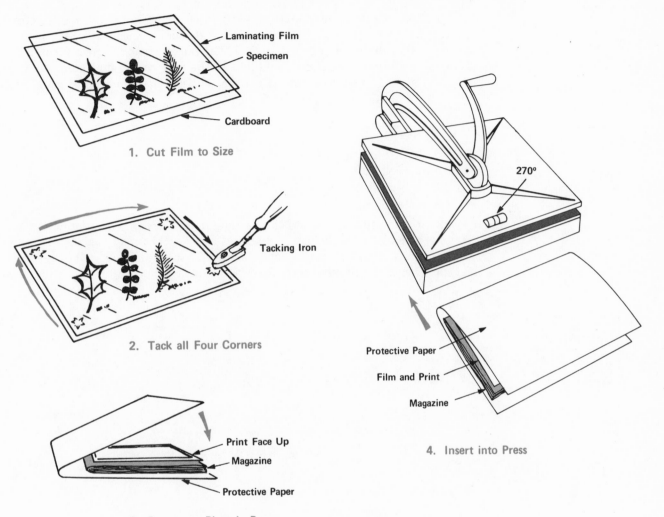

1. Cut Film to Size

2. Tack all Four Corners

3. Prepare to Place in Press

4. Insert into Press

seconds to "cook out" the moisture. Open the press and remove the specimen. Then:

1. Cut cardboard to size. Cut a piece of laminating plastic so it is *slightly smaller* than the cardboard mount. Position the specimen on top of the board and lay the heat-sensitive plastic *dull* side *down* on *top* of the specimen. If two or more specimens are mounted be sure the specimens are separated from each other, and that *no* specimen comes closer than 1/2" from the outer edges of the plastic.

2. Preheat the tacking iron (set at "hi") or the hand iron (set at "cotton"). Tack the plastic at all four corners, as illustrated, by touching the tip of the iron to the plastic for only an instant. Do *not* push the plastic toward the center of the board when tacking, as this will cause wrinkles in the finished lamination.

3. Place the mounting board on top of a magazine, and place both between the folds of a sheet of clean white paper.

4. Insert the assembled materials into the press. Leave them in the press for 15–30 seconds. Remove from the press and quickly place books on top

to prevent their warping during cooling. After the materials have cooled, trim the cardboard border off with a paper cutter or scissors. *Note:* If bubbles appear under the plastic, puncture or prick it with a straight pin or needle. Reinsert into the heated press to force the steam and air out. After 15 to 30 seconds remove from the press and quickly place weights on top. Allow to cool before removing weights. The tacking iron or a hand iron may be used to press the plastic down close to the edge of the specimen. Be sure to use a piece of paper on *top* of the plastic and *under* the iron to avoid the problem of plastic sticking to the iron.

Materials Sources

Glassoloid Corporation of America.
Sealamin: Seal, Inc.

RIKER MOUNTING

Riker mounting of materials has long been a favorite technique for arranging specimens for display and study. Any teacher may successfully employ this method to mount insect collections, Indian artifacts, coins, geological specimens, and other objects for use as instructional materials.

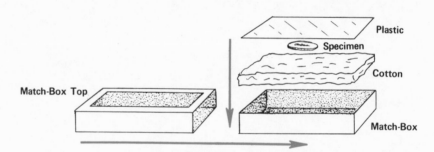

MATCH-BOX MOUNTING

Materials and Equipment

suitable shallow box
cellophane, Saran wrap, or clear acetate (plastic)
    cotton (preferably in roll form)
pins or thumbtacks
scissors
specimen to be mounted

Procedure

Cut the cotton to the desired size, usually slightly larger than the dimensions of the box. Place the cotton in the box, and pat into place. Cut a hole in the lid of the box 1″ from each edge. Turn the lid over, cut a piece of cellophane or clear plastic large enough to cover the opening, and tape it into place inside the lid with plastic or cellophane tape. Place the specimen in the box, lower the lid into place, and fasten with pins or thumbtacks on two or four sides. (*Note:* If desired, coat the specimen with plastic spray and allow to dry to make it more resistant to damage before placing into the box. Place a moth ball under the cotton to prevent moth damage if insects are to be mounted.)

Many types of small boxes may be used for Riker mounting. For small specimens, a match box works well (see the illustration). Small boxes need

RIKER MOUNTING

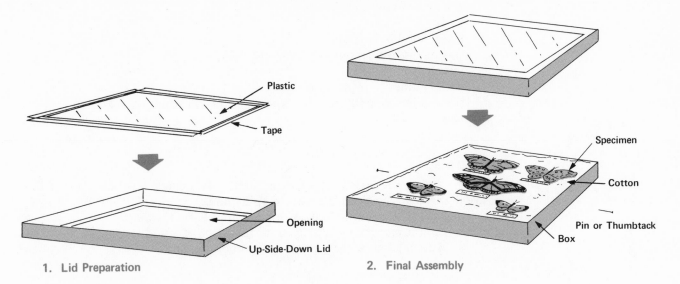

Plastic

Tape

Opening

Up-Side-Down Lid

1. Lid Preparation

Specimen

Cotton

Pin or Thumbtack

Box

2. Final Assembly

the lid holes cut closer to the edge than the 1″ mentioned above. It may be difficult to tape plastic inside a match-box cover; if so, tape the plastic over the opening on the outside.

INSECT-DISPLAY JAR

An insect-display jar allows for viewing specimens in the round. The jar provides relatively durable protection for specimens, shielding them from damage caused by atmospheric conditions or by active hands.

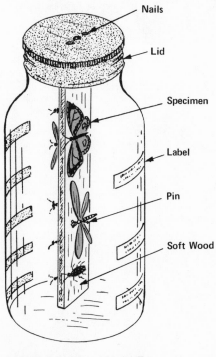

Nails

Lid

Specimen

Label

Pin

Soft Wood

INSECT-DISPLAY JAR

glass jar of appropriate size
jar lid
balsa wood or soft pine
specimens to be mounted, properly dried
insect pins
labels (adhesive if possible)
transparent tape (if adhesive labels are not available)
nails
hammer

Procedure

1. Fasten the wood slab to the jar lid by nailing into the end of the wood through the jar lid. To avoid splitting the wood, dull the tip of each nail slightly with a gentle blow of the hammer before nailing.
2. Pin the specimens in place onto the piece of wood.
3. Attach labels in the proper position on the jar.

GELATINE MOUNTING OF SPECIMENS

Gelatine mounting of specimens is especially useful for preservation and study of insects, starfish, sea horses, and other small, dry specimens. Teachers may easily accomplish useful, lasting mountings by this method.

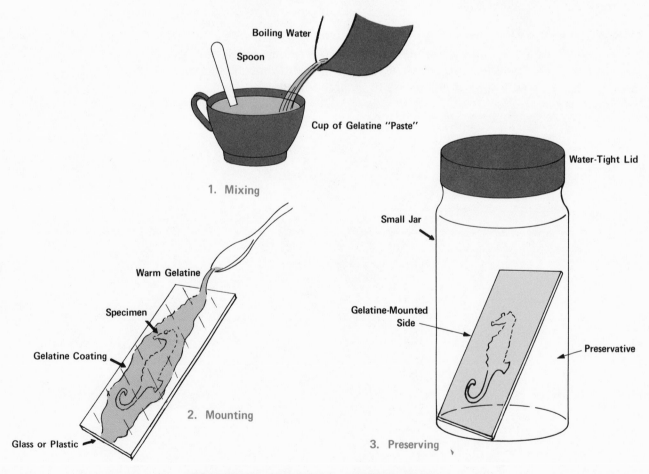

Boiling Water

Spoon

Cup of Gelatine "Paste"

1. Mixing

Water-Tight Lid

Small Jar

Warm Gelatine

Specimen

Gelatine Coating

Gelatine-Mounted Side

Preservative

Glass or Plastic

2. Mounting

3. Preserving

GELATINE MOUNTING OF SPECIMENS

unflavored clear gelatine
specimen to be mounted
small bottle with watertight lid
preservative (alcohol solution or formaldehyde)
strip of glass or plastic
spoon and container for mixing gelatine solution
pan of water and stove for heating water

Procedure

Previously dried specimens, such as insects, starfish, and sea horses, should be washed in cleaning fluid to remove grease. Place the specimen on a blotter to remove excess cleaning fluid. See "Drying Specimens" (page 56) if information is needed concerning how to dry insect specimens. Then:

1. Prepare gelatine according to the directions on the package.

2. Spoon gelatine over the specimen placed on a glass or plastic strip, and allow to harden.

3. Place the slide in a jar previously filled with preservative (alcohol solution or formaldehyde). Screw on a watertight lid. The specimen is now ready for repeated display, examination, and study. (*Note:* Reverse the cardboard lid liner if it is coated with wax, to avoid wax contamination of the preservative.)

EMBEDDING MATERIALS IN PLASTIC

Specimens properly embedded in plastic are preserved indefinitely; they are protected from deterioration through contact with air and moisture, and from damage through handling. If plastic in which materials have been embedded becomes scratched through repeated use, a light sanding and buffing restores the finish to its original utility and beauty. Materials embedded in plastic may be passed around the room for examination, placed on display, or projected in the opaque projector for all to see. Biological specimens, artifacts, coins, small photographs, and many other objects may profitably be preserved by this method. Supplies needed for embedding materials in plastic, complete with detailed instructions, are available directly from several commercial concerns.

Materials and Equipment

specimen, properly prepared (see "Drying Specimens," this section)
mold for forming and holding the plastic as it hardens (see step 1)
Bio-Plastic, Claro-Cast, or other special embedding plastics catalyst, prepared to make plastic harden or jell
medicine dropper for catalyst
mold-release compound for ease in removing embedded materials from molds
several grades of sandpaper, from No. 60 to No. 600
cellophane to cover the curing plastic
polishing agent (toothpaste or silver polish)
metal shears, vise, and file (needed for production of molds only)
oven (see step 5 for directions for making a homemade oven)

Procedure

Secure all necessary materials. Then:
1. Decide on the mold to be used. Cooking tins, small glass dishes, jars,

Thickness of Layer	Drops of Catalyst for Each Four Ounces of Plastic
Up to $\frac{1}{2}''$	35
$\frac{1}{2}''$ to $1''$	25
$1''$ to $2''$	12

or tin cans may be used. Aluminum strips, available as scraps from metal shops, may be cut with shears and bent to form molds convenient to use. To produce a small mold, cut a strip of aluminum scrap to $3\frac{1}{2}'' \times 2''$. Bend into a sharp "U" shape that has sides $\frac{3}{4}''$ high, and a bottom $2'' \times 2''$. Cut two scraps of metal or glass to $2\frac{1}{4}'' \times 2''$ to serve as sides of the mold. Fasten the components of the mold tightly together with a rubber band. Use other dimensions in constructing molds according to the size of the specimens to be embedded.

2. Mix enough plastic and catalyst to form a layer about one-third the thickness of the finished block. The plastic and catalyst may be mixed in a glass container or paper cups. Stir the plastic and catalyst with a spoon or glass rod. Be sure to use proportions of catalyst recommended by the manufacturer. When using Ward's Bio-Plastic, consult the table. Coat the interior of the mold with mold-release compound and pour the first, or supporting, layer of plastic. Take care to pop any air bubbles with a pin, or pull them off of the surface of the plastic with a medicine dropper. Allow the first layer to jell until it is firm enough to support the specimen. This may take several hours. Test to see if the plastic is jelling by pulling a pin across the surface of the plastic. If the layer is ready to receive a specimen, a thread of plastic will adhere to the pin. During the hardening period, cover the mold to prevent dust from settling on the surface of the plastic.

3. Place the specimen on the surface of the supporting layer of plastic. If necessary, anchor insect specimens into place with pins. Allow the specimen to adhere to the surface of the supporting layer of plastic for about 20 minutes. Remove pins and pour a second layer of plastic into the mold, thick enough to barely cover the specimen. Allow the second layer to harden before pouring the final layer of catalyzed plastic.

4. To help dissipate heat generated by the hardening process, place the mold in cool water as it jells. Allow the plastic to harden for several hours.

5. Cure the plastic by heating it in a oven at a temperature of $140°$ F. for three hours or more. If a metal oven is not available, construct an oven by inserting a 15-watt light bulb in a hole cut in the bottom of an oatmeal box. Place the mold on a board, put the oatmeal box oven over it, and turn on the light. After curing, allow to cool before removing from the oven. As it cools following oven heating, cover the tacky surface of the plastic with cellophane to make the surface more smooth and transparent.

6. After the plastic has cooled, remove the plastic block from the mold. Then remove cellophane and sand the surfaces of the plastic block where needed. Move progressively from coarse to fine sandpaper. Fine wet- or dry-type sandpaper moistened in water should be used for final sanding. Buffing and polishing may be done with toothpaste or silver polish.

DRYING SPECIMENS

Previously dried or dry specimens, such as insects, starfish, sea horses, shells, minerals, fossils, coins, and metals, should be washed in cleaning fluid to remove grease. Place the specimen on a blotter to remove excess cleaning fluid, and proceed with the embedding process.

EMBEDDING MATERIALS IN PLASTIC

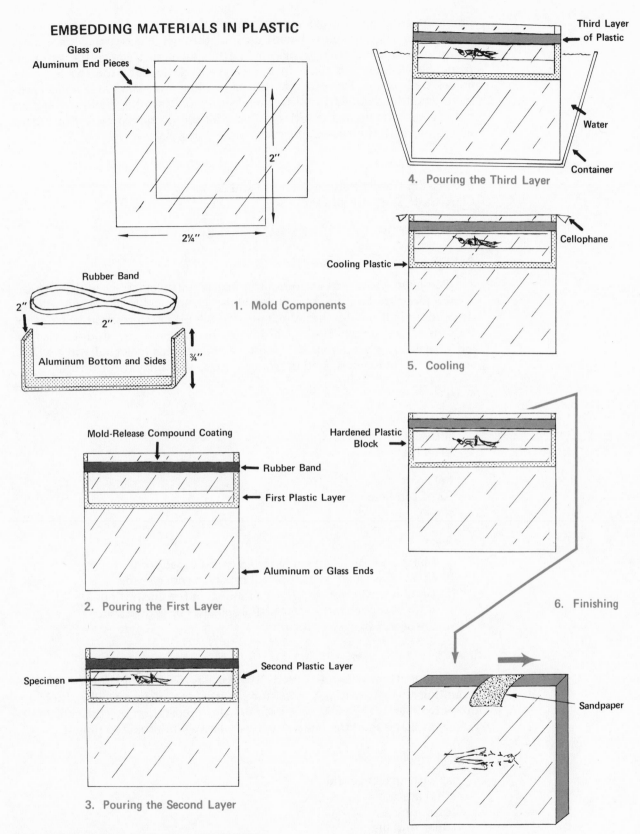

Glass or Aluminum End Pieces

2"

2¼"

1. Mold Components

Rubber Band

2"

2"

Aluminum Bottom and Sides

¾"

Mold-Release Compound Coating

Rubber Band

First Plastic Layer

Aluminum or Glass Ends

2. Pouring the First Layer

Specimen

Second Plastic Layer

3. Pouring the Second Layer

Third Layer of Plastic

Water

Container

4. Pouring the Third Layer

Cooling Plastic

Cellophane

5. Cooling

Hardened Plastic Block

6. Finishing

Sandpaper

TRANSPARENT OR CLEARED SPECIMEN

If internal structure of specimens such as embryos is to be studied, wash in water overnight, or throughout one day, to remove preserving fluid. Dehydrate the specimen by placing it in alcohol solutions. Move the specimen from water slightly diluted with alcohol through successive alcohol-water baths until the specimen is placed in 100% alcohol. Remove the specimen from the alcohol, and place in uncatalyzed plastic until the specimen becomes transparent. Proceed with the embedding process. (*Note:* Some specimens *must* be skinned prior to the clearing process.) Suggestions given are only representative of the variety of uses for plastic embedment. For further details, write to the manufacturers of embedding plastics.

Materials Sources

Bio-Plastic: Ward's Natural Science Establishment.
Claro-Cast: The Castolite Co.

DEVICES FOR CAPTURING AND KILLING SPECIMENS

BERLESE FUNNEL FOR CAPTURING SOIL FAUNA

The lamp above this assembly will provide sufficient heat to dry the soil. As the moisture level in the soil descends, the animal life in the soil will also descend and ultimately the animal life will fall into the preservative jar at the bottom of the funnel. The organisms can be observed and studied with the aid of a lens or a microscope. Most of the animals collected will be quite small and include mites, spiders, some worms, and some insect forms.

Materials

> funnel, metal
> fiberglass screening
> tin snips
> lamp
> bottle
> jar of formalin
> stapler

Procedure

1. Shape a piece of screening into a cone-shaped form.
2. Staple the screen so that it will retain the cone shape.
3. Complete the Berlese funnel as shown in the illustration.
4. Fill the funnel and screen with a spadeful of garden soil.
5. Suspend a light over the dirt.

INSECT-KILLING JAR

Various techniques are used by teachers for killing insects prior to mounting them for display and study. One type of insect-killing bottle is presented here. The materials used in the preparation of this bottle are readily available, and the killing agent is relatively nontoxic to humans.

Materials and Equipment

> jar with an airtight lid
> ethyl acetate
> teaspoon
> paper toweling
> light cardboard
> cotton
> scissors

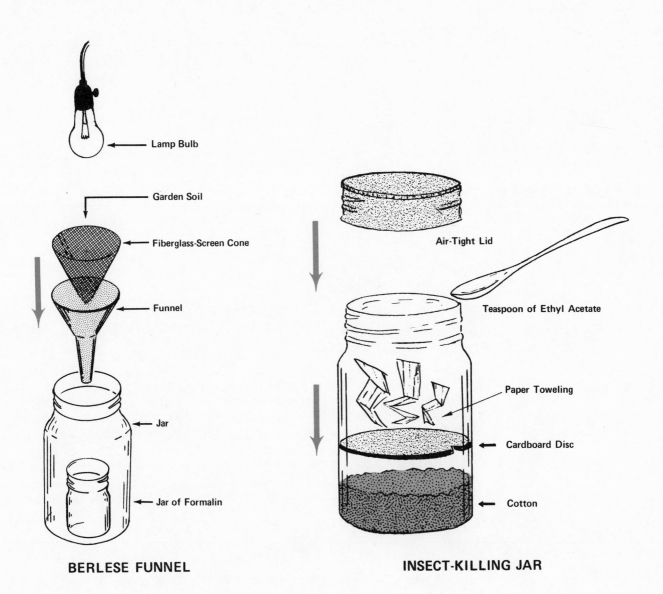

Lamp Bulb

Garden Soil

Fiberglass-Screen Cone

Funnel

Jar

Jar of Formalin

Air-Tight Lid

Teaspoon of Ethyl Acetate

Paper Toweling

Cardboard Disc

Cotton

BERLESE FUNNEL

INSECT-KILLING JAR

Procedure

Secure the materials needed. Then:

Wad the cotton to a depth of approximately ³/₄″, in the bottom of the jar. Cut a circle of cardboard a little larger than the diameter of the jar, then cut a notch in the edge of the cardboard circle. Force the cardboard into the jar, and press it firmly down against the cotton layer.

Tilt the jar on its side and pour a teaspoon of ethyl acetate down the inside of the jar. Wipe out the inside of the jar after the ethyl acetate has run down into the cotton layer. Insert strips of paper toweling cut to a width of 1″ and screw the lid on tight once more. Recharge the jar before each field trip by pouring in additional quantities of ethyl acetate.

Other types of insect-killing jars may be easily produced by the teacher, and other agents used (including gasoline and cleaning fluids); however, if children are handling insect-killing jars, care should be taken to use agents which are relatively nontoxic to humans.

Lettering
Instructional
Materials

III

To be most effective, displays, charts, graphs, bulletin boards, and other visual materials often must be accompanied by verbal explanations. Lettering quality and the legibility of accompanying labels and captions can add to or detract from the effectiveness of any display, and thus facilitate or limit learning from instructional materials.

General suggestions for lettering, plus a discussion of lettering pens, lettering systems and guides, dry transfer and acetate letters, three-dimensional letters, flat opaque letters, and lettering for special effects are presented here.

GENERAL SUGGESTIONS

Some suggestions which teachers should keep in mind when lettering instructional materials include:

1. Keep labels and captions short and simple. Don't use unnecessary verbiage; be crisp and to the point.

2. Lettering style should be simple. Don't use fancy letters; use a style that is easy to read.

3. Use a uniform height in lettering materials. Horizontal guide lines, drawn lightly with a pencil, may be useful in keeping lettering straight and uniform.

4. Spacing of letters should be done optically. Estimate space needed for lettering by counting spaces, leaving two to four spaces between words; then, adjust the estimate by allowing $1^{1}/_{4}$ spaces for M and W, and $^{1}/_{4}$ space for I.

5. Generally, it is best to allow about $1^{1}/_{4}$ to $1^{1}/_{2}$ times the height of the caption line as spacing measurement between successive lines of lettering.

6. Be sure captions can be read from a distance when used on displays.

7. In lettering projection materials, such as overhead transparencies, care must be taken to see that the letters are large enough to be easily read when projected on the screen. Tecnifax Corporation has developed a template, reproduced full size here, which may serve as a guide for lettering on projection materials. This template is available, full size and printed on plastic, from Tecnifax Corporation.

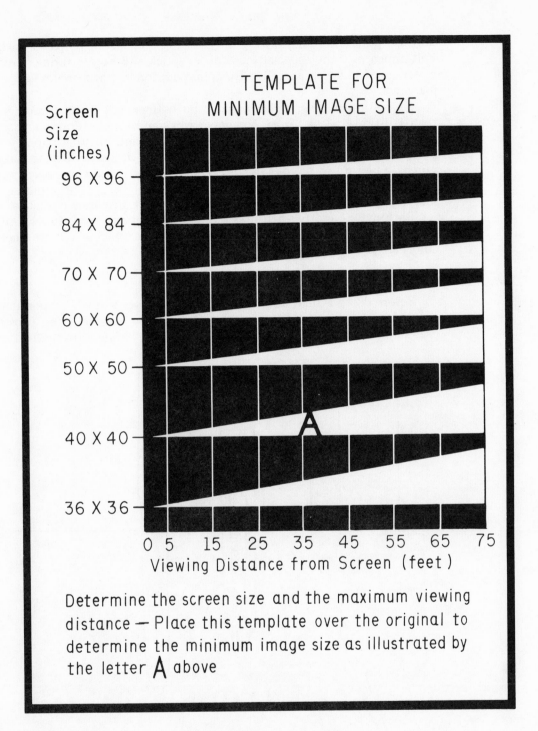

TEMPLATE FOR MINIMUM IMAGE SIZE

Screen Size (inches)

96 X 96
84 X 84
70 X 70
60 X 60
50 X 50
40 X 40
36 X 36

0 5 15 25 35 45 55 65 75
Viewing Distance from Screen (feet)

Determine the screen size and the maximum viewing distance — Place this template over the original to determine the minimum image size as illustrated by the letter A above

LETTERING PENS

Various types of lettering pens are available to help teachers do a more effective, professional job of lettering instructional materials. Three kinds of easy-to-use, inexpensive lettering pens that teachers have found effective are felt-tipped and nylon-tipped pens, Speedball pens, and duck-bill (metal-brush) pens.

FELT-TIPPED AND NYLON-TIPPED PENS

Felt-tipped pens are available with a variety of points suitable for fine- or wide-line drawing and lettering purposes. Instant-drying inks in many colors may be purchased for drawing on glass, plastic, metal, or paper surfaces. Felt-tipped pens are especially useful for quick and easy lettering of display materials of all types, as well as for color addition to transparency-projection materials.

Nylon-tipped pens typically have much finer and more durable points than felt-tipped pens. Thus, for detail work and fine lettering in preparing transparencies, nylon-tipped pens are often excellent. For transparency work be sure you use pens suitable for writing on glass or plastic. Before making a purchase be sure to *try out* the pen by drawing or writing on a piece of glass or plastic. If the ink "beads up," it is not suitable. If a continuous smooth line results it will probably work satisfactorily on transparency plastics.

Both nylon- and felt-pen inks may *not* project true color tones. Only by projecting the color onto a screen will it be possible to tell whether the colors are as desired.

Procedure

Before doing a final lettering job, sketch a layout of the proposed material and practice your lettering on scrap material. Always clean pens after use, and be sure to cover the felt tips of the pens before putting them away.

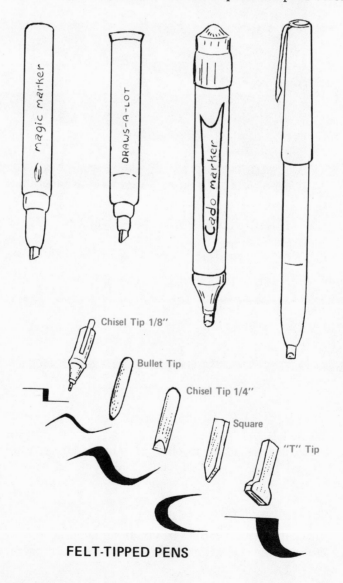

Chisel Tip 1/8"

Bullet Tip

Chisel Tip 1/4"

Square

"T" Tip

FELT-TIPPED PENS

Cushman and Denison Manufacturing Co.
Eugene Dietzgen Co.
Marsh Stencil Co.

SPEEDBALL PENS

When small or medium-sized letters are needed, consider using a Speed-ball pen. Pen points are available from $\frac{1}{4}''$ wide (size 0) to the finest line (size 6). Four styles of points may be purchased for doing various lettering jobs. Both pen size and style are imprinted on top of each pen point.

Procedure

Teachers should practice lettering with various Speedball points before attempting finished lettering on displays. After satisfactory skill has been developed, and a point has been selected for the job at hand, do a practice layout to check spacing and placement of letters. Be sure to touch the point of the pen to a piece of scratch paper to remove excess ink before drawing letters.

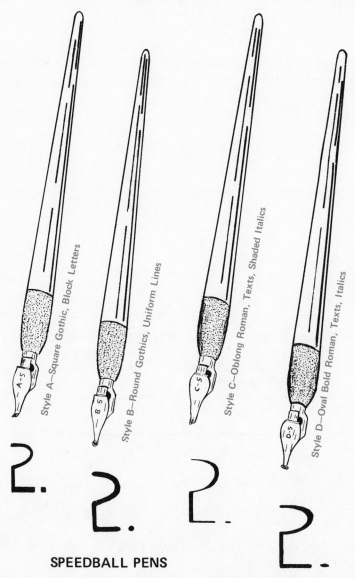

SPEEDBALL PENS

Drawlet Pens (similar to Speedball): The Esterbrook Co.
Speedball Pens: Arthur Brown & Bro., Inc.

DUCK-BILL STEEL-BRUSH PENS

Duck-bill steel-brush pens are especially useful for fast, clean lettering of posters, charts, graphs, and other display materials when a medium or large letter is needed. These pens may be used for the application of India inks, plastic inks, oils, water colors, and paints. Four pen widths are available: $3/8''$, $1/2''$, $3/4''$, and $1/4''$.

Procedure

When using steel-brush pens, teachers will find it is advantageous to use a T-square or ruler with a raised edge to help make lettering straight and neat. Block lettering is especially easy to do with steel-brush pens.

Materials Source

Steel Brush Pens: Arthur Brown & Bro., Inc.

STENCILS

Stencils are inexpensive, durable, and easy to use for making attractive letters for charts, posters, and other materials. Letter outlines are often done

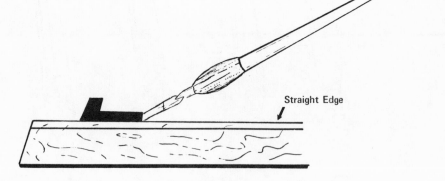

DUCK-BILL STEEL-BRUSH PENS

STENCILS

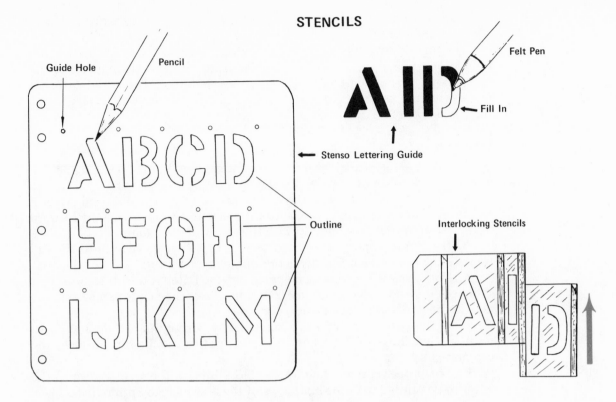

Guide Hole | Pencil | Felt Pen | Fill In | Stenso Lettering Guide | Outline | Interlocking Stencils

through openings in the stencil directly on the display material with a pencil, and later filled in with a brush, felt-tipped pen, or other coloring device.

Stenso lettering guides are easy to use and are available in letter size from ½" to 8", in Gothic, Roman, and Old English, both upper and lower case. Stenso guides have special guide holes which make spacing and alignment of letters very easy.

Metal interlocking stencils are available which are especially useful when words are to be repeatedly used in lettering a chart or several charts. Words can be made up and used over and over, then easily taken apart when they are no longer needed. Care must be taken when using paints or inks with metal guides, for some inks tend to run under the metal stencils. Quick-drying inks and thick paints work best when using metal guides; paints should be applied with quick, dabbing motions.

Interlocking metal stencils can be obtained from Krengel Manufacturing Company, Inc., 227 Fulton Street, New York, N.Y. 10007. The materials source for Stenso lettering guides is the Stenso Lettering Company, 1101 E. 25th Street, Baltimore, Maryland 21218.

LETTERING SYSTEMS AND GUIDES

UNIMARK SYSTEM

The Unimark System[1] provides an inexpensive way to quickly and easily make labels on tape for use on charts or maps, or for use on any other smooth surface where easy-to-read larger lettering is needed. Transparent tape is also available for making labels and lettering for transparencies suitable for use on the overhead projector. A Unimark System kit is an excellent

---

[1] Uniline Corporation, 33450 Western Avenue, Union City, California 94587.

investment for a teacher wishing to prepare professional-appearing letters at a reasonable cost.

The tape is available in 1″ or ½″ widths. A single line of ⅝″ letters or a double line of ⅜″ or ¼″ letters can be made on 1″-width tape. The ½″ tape allows for a single row of ⅜″ or ¼″ lettering. The ⅝″ lettering is made with the pen marked LARGE. The ⅜″ or ¼″ lettering is made with the pen marked SMALL.

Procedure

1. Clip the tape cartridge onto the right-hand end of the lettering device, as in the illustration of the assembled system.

2. Load the tape, feeding the end of the tape into the slot until it meets resistance. Turn the knob at the rear of the machine to feed the tape forward until the end of the tape lines up with the arrow marked *tape*.

3. Insert the appropriate scale. The ⅝″ letter scale slides into the full track or the inside track for single- or double-line lettering.

4. The black line on the scale preceding the letter you wish to print first should line up with the arrow marked *print*. Press the pen firmly against the tape in the *upright* (perpendicular) position.

5. If the pen does not write immediately, shake the pen up and down until the ink flows freely. When the pen is not in use, be sure to place the cap on tightly.

6. For proper spacing, line up the black line on the scale preceding the letter to be printed with the *right edge* of the letter already printed. To space between words use the space of an "average" letter. If the message is longer than the "printing bed," simply advance the tape by turning the knob and continue printing.

7. Cut the tape by turning the cutter at the end of the machine in a complete *counterclockwise* circle. Peel off the backing, and press into place on a clean surface. *Note:* Several letters are made by combining strokes in two steps.

LABEL MAKER

Several label-embossing devices are currently on the market for the preparation of self-adhesive labels to be used in identifying books, instructional materials, and other items.

When purchasing a label maker, be sure you buy one which is durable enough to stand up under school use. A little more money spent to insure quality will pay off handsomely in trouble-free use. Use of Dymo M-10/14[2] is described as the typical equipment suitable for use in schools.

Procedure

Select a label maker and tape of appropriate width. Machines that will print two widths of tape, usually ⅜″ and ¼″, are preferable. Then:

1. Set the tape selector pin (A) *up* for ¼″ tape, *down* for ⅜″ tape. Select a tape magazine, and pull out about 3″ of tape. Open the tape-chute cover (B).

2. Slip the U-shaped opening of the magazine (C) into the top of the tape channel and push forward and down until it locks into place.

3. Thread the front of the tape into the ⅜″ or ¼″ slot (D) until the tape engages in the feed roller. Close the tape-chute lid.

---

[2] Dymo Products Co.

UNIMARK LETTERING SYSTEM

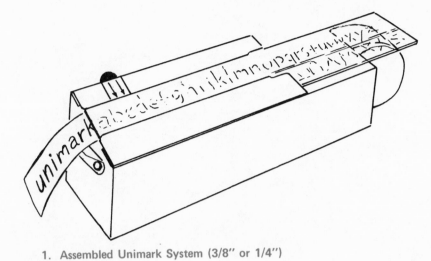

1. Assembled Unimark System (3/8" or 1/4")

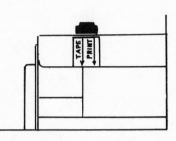

2. Load Tape

5/8" Lettering Scale

3/8" Lettering Scale

1/4" Lettering Scale

3. Insert Scale

4. Start Lettering

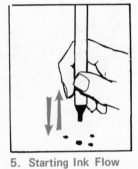

5. Starting Ink Flow

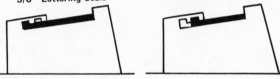

6. Spacing

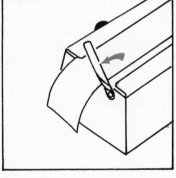

7. Cutting Tape

4. Turn the tape-advance knob (E) counterclockwise until about ¼" of the tape extends past the front of the tool.

5. Pull up the cut-off lever (F) and remove the small piece of cut-off tape.

6. Dial the embossing wheel (G) until the desired letter appears in the letter-selection slot.

7. Squeeze the embossing handle (H) *firmly up into the machine*. Release. To space between words, squeeze the embossing handle gently *only*

LABEL MAKER

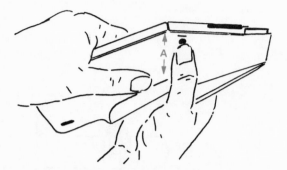

1. Select Tape Width (3/8" or 1/4")

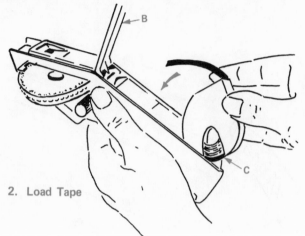

2. Load Tape

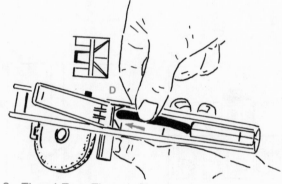

3. Thread Tape Through Slot

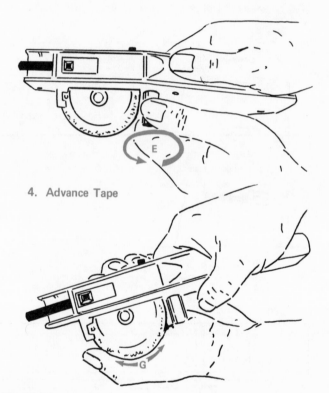

4. Advance Tape

5. Trim End

6. Dial Letter

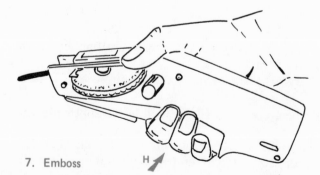

7. Emboss

LABEL MAKER

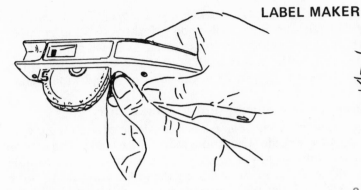

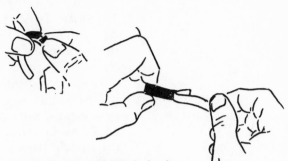

8. Advance; Cut

9. Peel Backing off Label; Apply

until you hear a click, no farther, then release, and then select and emboss your next letter. To back up the tape, squeeze the embossing handle *gently* until you hear a click, retain in that position, then turn the tape-advance knob clockwise.

8. After you have completed your last letter, advance the tape with the tape-advance knob until the last letter is aligned with the cut-off guide lines at the top front of the tool. Pull up the cut-off lever *firmly*. Release the lever, and pull the label out of the machine. The machine is now ready to use for making another label. Your message is now centered on the tape. Notice the small tab at the right end of the label—this facilitates removal of the tape's protective backing strip.

9. Hold the tape by the edges to avoid touching the adhesive. Pull down the tab end of the tape to strip off the protective backing. To apply the label, first stick down one end and then roll the label down. Rub the label briskly with your thumb.

RAPIDOGRAPH SYSTEM

Rapidograph pens and Rapidoguides are relatively easy to use, and not nearly as expensive as most other systems. Many teachers purchase two guide and pen sets, one appropriate for drawing $5/8''$ letters, and a second for $3/16''$ letters. These guides will suffice for most lettering done on transparencies, for transparency masters, for labels on study prints (pictures) and maps, and for directions on displays prepared for learning and study centers. For larger letters, other systems should be considered.

Materials and Equipment

> Rapidoguides
> straight edge (a T-square or ruler will be satisfactory)
> masking or drafting tape and pins
> drawing ink suitable for paper or plastic (Pelican or Koh-i-noor inks are
>   excellent)
> Rapidograph pens or equivalent
> paper, cardboard, or plastic drawing surface
> paper towel, one end moistened
> flat working surface (table or drafting board)
> scrap paper

Procedure

Check to see if the pen is filled with ink and ready to use. Shake it up and down a few times to get the ink to flow. Test for flow on a piece of scrap paper. If necessary, fill the pen. If using a Rapidograph pen, take off the plunger cover located above the color-code ring by twisting *counterclockwise*. Twist the plunger counterclockwise as far as it will go. Insert the tip of the pen in the ink bottle, and twist the plunger *clockwise*. Ink will be sucked into the pen. Remove the pen from the ink bottle and wipe it clean with a moist paper towel.

Tape or pin the copy to the working surface at the corners.

Place the Rapidoguide on the copy, then position the straight edge against the *lower* edge of the guide. Use a tape loop (illustrated in the section on Leroy Lettering Systems, page 74) or strips of tape at each end to hold the straight edge in place. Position the guide so the letter you wish to begin with is over the copy. Hold the pen *perpendicular to the copy*, insert the point into the guide, and begin lettering. After a letter is completed, lift out the pen, move the guide over to the next letter, and proceed. The guide should be raised off the copy surface to prevent smearing. Spacing is done by considering *area* between letters rather than *distance*. (Two curved lines opposite each other are spaced closer together than two vertical lines, for example).

Additional Information

1. Ink-filled pens should *always* be tightly capped when not in use. A special humidor may be purchased for pen storage which will help to keep pens from drying out and clogging.

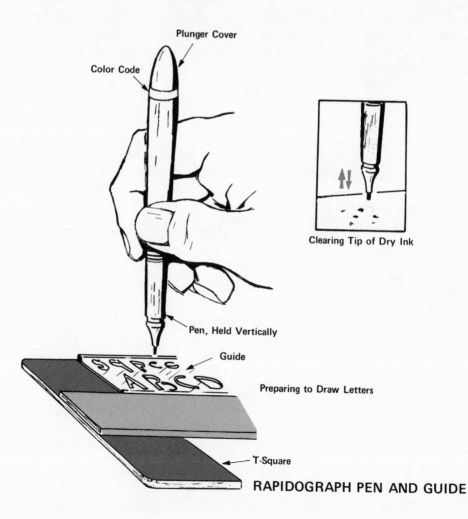

Plunger Cover

Color Code

Clearing Tip of Dry Ink

Pen, Held Vertically

Guide

Preparing to Draw Letters

T-Square

RAPIDOGRAPH PEN AND GUIDE

KOH-I-NOOR RAPIDOGUIDES: GUIDE NUMBERS, PEN NUMBERS, AND SPECIMEN LETTERS (FROM THE MANUFACTURER'S LITERATURE)

Guide No.			Specimen Letters
3030/A	**Rapidoguide** 5/64" FOR USE WITH **RAPIDOGRAPH** No. 00		for swift sure lettering, use KOH-I-NOOR RAPIDOGUIDES ABCDEGHIJKLMNOPQRSTUVW abcdefghijklmnopqrstuvwxyz
3030/B	**Rapidoguide** 1/8" FOR USE WITH **RAPIDOGRAPH** No. 00		for swift sure lettering, use KOH-I-NOOR RAPIDOGUIDES ABCDEGHIJKLMNOPQRSTUVW
3030	**Rapidoguide** 5/32" FOR USE WITH **RAPIDOGRAPH** No. 0		for swift sure lettering, use KOH-I-NOOR RAPIDOGUIDES
3031	**Rapidoguide** 3/16" FOR USE WITH **RAPIDOGRAPH** No. 1		for swift, sure lettering KOH-I-NOOR RAPIDOG
3032	**Rapidoguide** 1/4" FOR USE WITH **RAPIDOGRAPH** No. 2		for swift, sure lett KOH-I-NOOR RAPI
3032/A	**Rapidoguide** 9/32" FOR USE WITH **RAPIDOGRAPH** No. 2½		for swift, sure let KOH-I-NOOR RAP
3033	**Rapidoguide** 5/16" FOR USE WITH **RAPIDOGRAPH** No. 3		for swift, KOH-I
3034	**Rapidoguide** 3/8" FOR USE WITH **RAPIDOGRAPH** No. 4		for swift, KOH

2. Clogged pens may be soaked in warm water to which detergent is added. Let them soak *overnight*, and clean.

3. Several other makes of technical drawing pens may be used with Rapidoguides (Mars technical pens, for example). Be sure pen-point widths and Rapidoguides are compatible before purchasing.

Materials Source

Koh-i-noor, Inc.

Wrico Signmaker guides and the appropriate pens are used for making larger letters on charts, posters, and for lettering captions for bulletin-board displays. Lettering from $1/2''$ to $4''$ in height can be produced using the unit.

Components necessary for completing letters with this system include a stencil guide, a special brush pen or felt pen, and a guide holder.

Materials and Equipment

stencil guide
brush pen or felt pen
guide holder
hard-finished paper or cardboard
clean, firm working surface
paper toweling or tissue
drawing ink, good quality

Procedure

1. Select the stencil guide needed by reading the code printed at center below the stencil openings. The code will indicate the letter style and whether the letters are capitals or lower case, their height, and the pen needed to complete the lettering. For example, for lettering $1 1/2''$ in height the following code might be printed in the guide: GUIDE NO. AVC 150. AV refers to the style; C indicates capitals or upper case; 150 gives the letter height ($1.50''$ or $1 1/2''$). For other letter heights the code reads as follows: $100 = 1''$, $75 = 3/4''$, etc. You will also find printed on the guide an instruction like USE WITH BRUSH PEN C OR FELT PEN NCF. This means to use a C-width pen. Be *sure* you use the specified pen, for the pen you use is critical.

2. Select the pen needed. The brush pens will have an engraved letter near the tip—A through E, narrow through wide—indicating width of line.

3. Adjust the brush pen so the brush is *slightly recessed* by holding the collar (see illustration) while twisting the barrel of the pen until the desired adjustment is completed.

4. Turn the guide holder over and read the instructions on the back. Return to the upright position, and place on the copy to be lettered. Insert the guide into the holder using the appropriate side.

5. Fill the pen by depressing the plunger and inserting the brush into the ink bottle. Wipe off the excess ink with a paper towel, after allowing the brush to retract into the barrel. Touch the tip of the pen to scrap paper to prepare the flow.

6. Insert the pen into the guide, holding it perpendicular (vertically) in relation to the copy. Use a firm grip on the pen, but do *not* exert much pressure on the paper; too much pressure will cause damage to the paper and stop the even flow of ink. You may go over a letter more than once. It is best to start near the middle of the opening and work toward either end of the letter being made.

Spacing is done optically, considering area between letters rather than distance. A little practice will help you decide how you should proceed on the final effort. Be sure to depress the brush and rinse under running water to clean after use.

If felt pens are used, follow the guide openings, holding the pen perpendicular to the copy. Do not rinse after use. Keep the pens tightly capped when not in use. Since felt pens are more expensive to use than brush pens, brush pens are more appropriate for general use.

WRICO SIGNMAKER PEN AND GUIDE

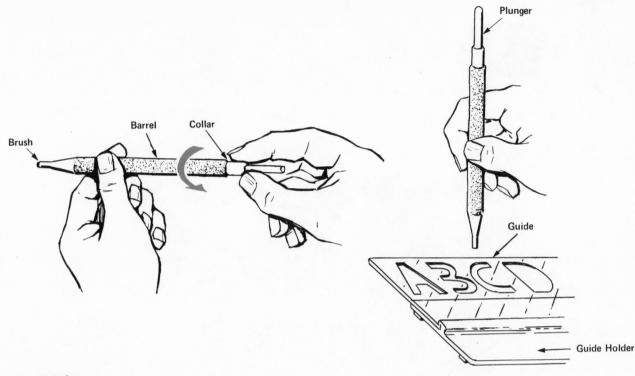

Materials Source

Wood-Regan Instrument Co.

WRICO STANDARD PENS AND GUIDES

For *small* letters suitable for picture labels, transparency masters (originals) and other similar jobs, Wrico Standard pens and guides are very useful and yield professional results with practice.

The Wrico Standard pen should be used with the Wrico Standard or Wrico-Print guide. Interchangeable points are available for different lettering purposes. Be sure to hold the pen in a vertical position when lettering to avoid spilling ink and to insure even, neat lettering.

Materials Source

Wood-Regan Instrument Co.

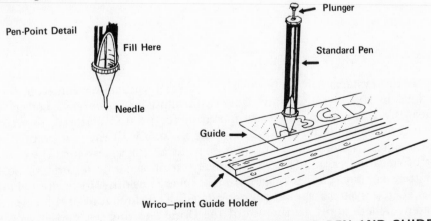

WRICO STANDARD PEN AND GUIDE

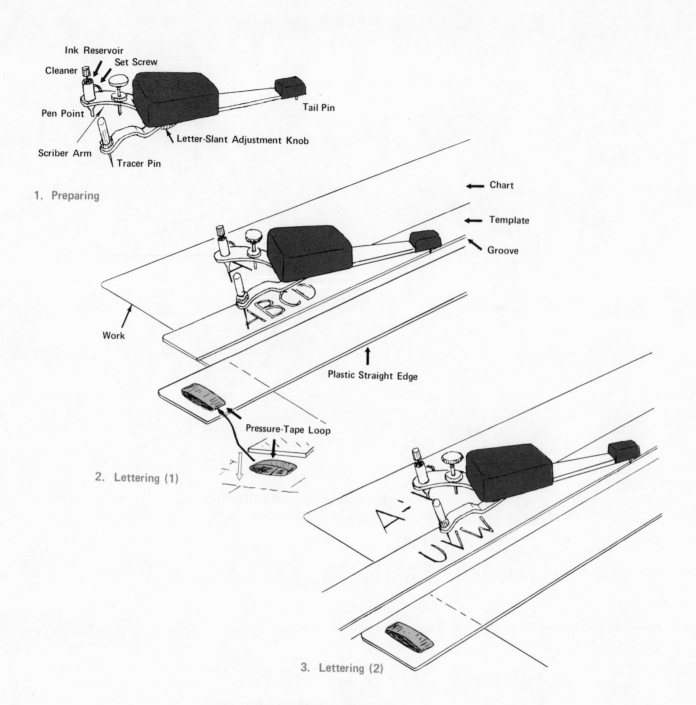

Ink Reservoir
Set Screw
Cleaner
Pen Point
Scriber Arm
Tracer Pin
Letter-Slant Adjustment Knob
Tail Pin

1. Preparing

Chart
Template
Groove

Work

Plastic Straight Edge

Pressure-Tape Loop

2. Lettering (1)

3. Lettering (2)

LEROY LETTERING SYSTEMS

Leroy systems can enable teachers to draw vertical or slanted letters of various heights, widths, and styles with consistent accuracy. Letters produced by this system often are mistaken for printed material, due to the perfection of the lettering job. Lettering is done with the pen point free of the template, leaving the printing in view at all times, lessening the possibility of smearing or smudging. If relatively small, accurate lettering is needed for transparency masters (page 7), maps, charts, or other instructional materials, Leroy systems should be considered. The directions and illustrations presented here apply to the use of the Doric lettering set, chosen as representative of inexpensive Leroy lettering systems.

Secure all needed supplies and equipment. Then:

1. Select the pen giving desired width of line (for letter size 100 and 140, pen 8910C; letter size 240, pen 8910E). Insert the pen in the pen socket at the end of the scriber arm and tighten set screw. Fill the reservoir with lettering ink.

2. Fasten a straight edge in place on the working surface with bands of masking tape (adhesive side out) under each end as illustrated. Slide material to be lettered under the straight edge at this time. Place a template with the desired size of letters along the straight edge, and place the tail pin of the scriber in the long straight groove of the template. Select the letter to be drawn and place the tracer pin on the template in the lowest part of the letter. Move the template and scriber until the pen point is directly over the copy where the first letter is to be drawn and draw the first letter.

3. With the pen clear of the drawing, move the scriber to the next letter and slide the template along the straight edge until the pen is over the position for the next letter. Draw the next letter, holding the template in place as the pen point moves over the drawing surface. Continue until the first line of lettering is completed.

When the pen is filled with ink, be sure to keep it in a vertical position to avoid spilling ink. When not in use, rest the scriber arm so as to keep the pen point clear of the working surface. Lift the cleaner slightly to start the flow of ink if the scriber has been standing idle for some time. Be sure to blot the point of the pen tip before beginning lettering. Clean the pen after each use with running water to prevent the clogging of the tip.

Materials Source

Keuffel and Esser Co.

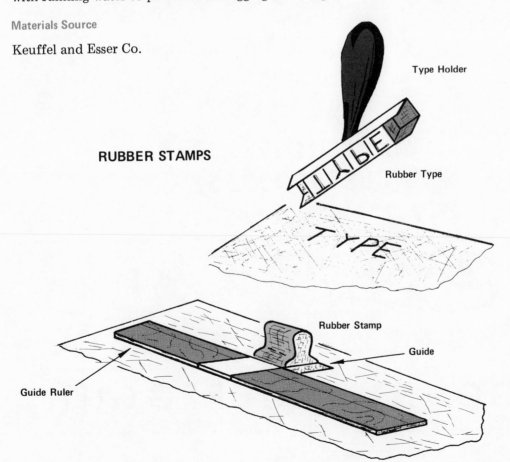

RUBBER STAMPS

Type Holder

Rubber Type

Rubber Stamp

Guide

Guide Ruler

RUBBER STAMPS

Rubber-stamp lettering kits are available to help make lettering quick and easy by printing complete words on instructional materials in one easy operation. Simply assemble the type in the type holder (both single- and multi-type styles are available), press down on the ink pad, and stamp the desired lettering on the art work.

When doing larger lettering jobs, it may be desirable to use individual letters or common letter combinations that are available with individual handles permanently attached to the rubber type. These letters are lined up on a vertical guide that is attached to a guide ruler. As lettering is done, the vertical guide is moved along the guide ruler to allow for spacing, which is properly done when the trailing edge of the stamp is lined up with the edge of the preceding letter.

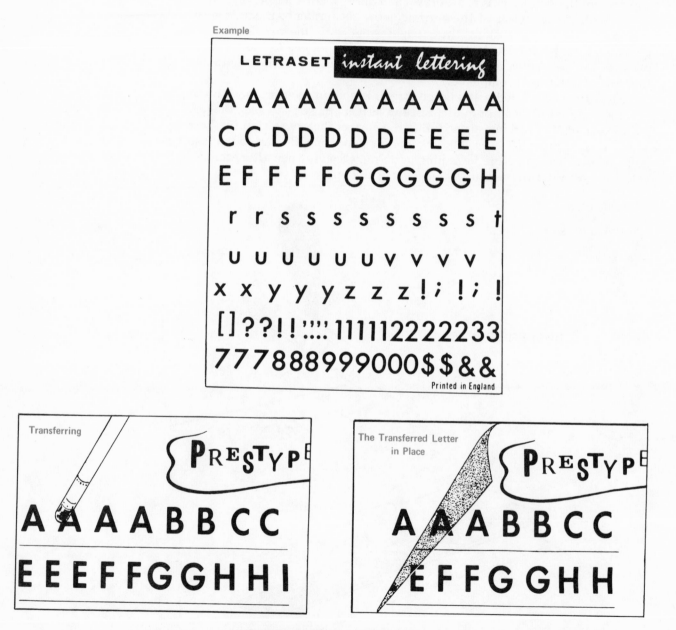

DRY-TRANSFER LETTERING

Beckley-Cardy Co.
Horder's.
Krengel Manufacturing Co.

LETTERS, SYMBOLS, AND TAPES

In this section we will discuss the following quite effective, commercially prepared letters, symbols, and tapes: printed-acetate (plastic) charting tapes, dry-transfer lettering, adhesive pictorial charting symbols, and printed-acetate (plastic) charting tapes.

DRY-TRANSFER LETTERING

A method of quick lettering, available under such trade names as Instant Lettering and Prestype, has found increasing favor among commercial artists, draftsmen, and teachers.

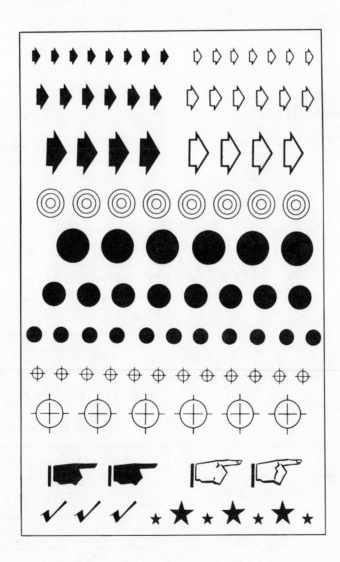

DRY-TRANSFER SYMBOLS-EXAMPLES

Procedure

Each letter, on a backing sheet, is placed on the spot where needed. Pressure—applied by rubbing on the backing sheet (which is on top of the letters) directly over the letter with the end of a ball-point pen, stylus, or rounded stick—will transfer the letter quickly and easily to the art work. A variety of symbols for dry transfer are also available. Some of these symbols are shown to acquaint teachers with what is available in this regard.

Materials Sources

Instant Lettering: Arthur Brown & Bro., Inc.
Prestype: Prestype, Inc.

PRINTED-ACETATE (PLASTIC) LETTERING SHEETS

Several companies produce self-adhering, printed-acetate sheets of letters, numbers, symbols, borders, screens, and shading mediums. One of these, Artype, is presented as an example of a superior product useful for lettering materials of all types. The dry, nonsticky pressure-sensitive adhesive on the back of Artype sheets makes the application of letters clean and simple.

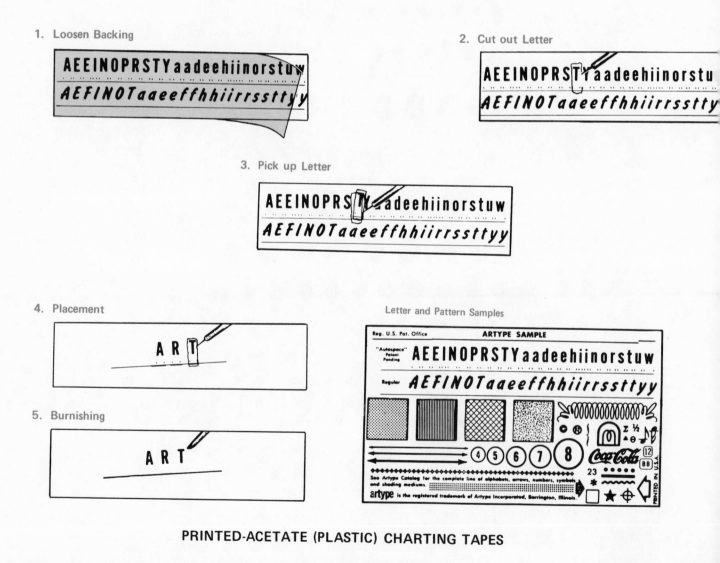

1. Loosen Backing

2. Cut out Letter

3. Pick up Letter

4. Placement

5. Burnishing

Letter and Pattern Samples

PRINTED-ACETATE (PLASTIC) CHARTING TAPES

Procedure

Complete the project except for lettering. Then:

1. Lay the Artype sheet *face down*, and loosen the backing sheet from the Artype as illustrated. Drop the backing sheet back onto the Artype sheet.

2. Draw a lettering guide line on the art work. (*Note:* In the case of transparencies, draw a guide line on a sheet of paper, position the paper under the transparent sheet, and fasten the paper and transparency together temporarily with a paper clip or tape.) With a stylus, cut around the letter to be used, being sure to include the guide line printed below it. Do *not* cut through the backing sheet.

3. Lift the letter from the backing sheet with the point of the stylus.

4. Position the letter on the chart or transparency, placing the Artype guide line in register with the guide line of the chart. Burnish *lightly* with the beveled end of the stylus.

5. When all lettering is laid out on the art work, make any changes needed in spacing or alignment, and burnish all letters *firmly* into place (but *not* the printed guide lines) until all edges disappear. Cut away the guide lines with the point of the stylus and burnish where needed.

Materials Source

Artype, Inc.

ADHESIVE PICTORIAL CHARTING SYMBOLS

Symbols backed with adhesive and printed on white opaque paper stock are available for use in symbolizing numerical quantity for comparative purposes in chart work. Symbols are available which indicate people, various animals, industrial concerns, various mining properties, gas and oil production, ships, farms, and buildings. Teachers also have a choice in symbol size. One kind of symbol sheet, Pictograph, is especially easy to use, and is illustrated here.

Pictograph Symbols

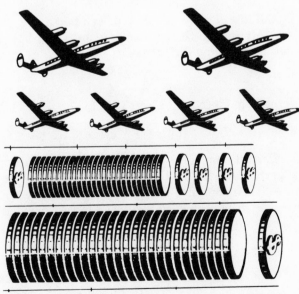

ADHESIVE PICTORIAL CHARTING SYMBOLS

ADHESIVE PICTORIAL CHARTING SYMBOLS

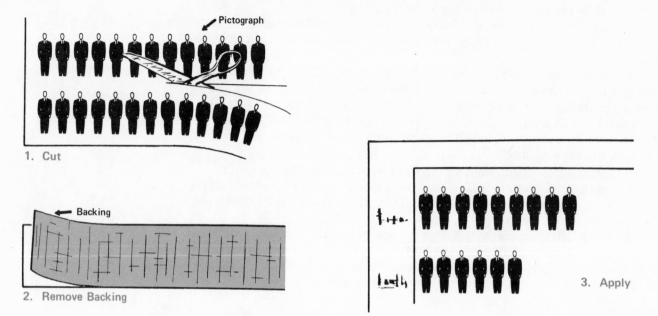

1. Cut

2. Remove Backing

3. Apply

Suggestions for Using Pictorial Symbols

    1. Numerical differences are best indicated by using different numbers of symbols, rather than by using symbols of different size (larger symbols with smaller symbols).

    2. Pictorial symbols are used to present an over-all picture, not minute detail. Use fractions of symbols sparingly.

    3. Pictorial symbols are most effective when used to present quantitative comparisons, rather than isolated facts.

    4. Symbols should look like the objects they stand for.

Procedure

    Cut the desired number of symbols from the symbol line of the sheet. Strip off the protective backing sheet and position the symbol line on the chart. Rub firmly into place.

Materials Source

Pictograph, Picto-Pak: Chart-Pak, Inc.

PRINTED-ACETATE (PLASTIC) CHARTING TAPES

    Several companies now produce printed acetate tapes useful for all types of graphic work. One brand of tape, Chart-Pak, is presented as an example of an excellent product for the application of symbols, borders, and graph lines to instructional materials of all kinds. Chart-Pak is available printed on an opaque or transparent plastic base.

Procedure

    Complete the project except for the addition of tape. Then:

    1. Unroll a short length of the pattern or color to be applied. Allow the end of the tape to overlap the starting point (see illustration) about 1″. Lay the tape on the desired area and press carefully into place.

PRINTED-ACETATE (PLASTIC) CHARTING TAPES

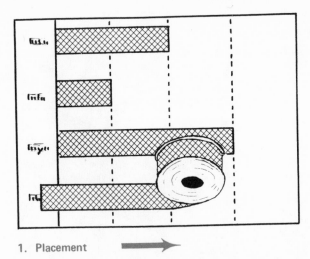

1. Placement

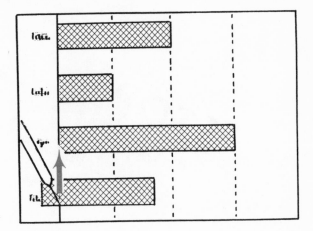

2. Trimming

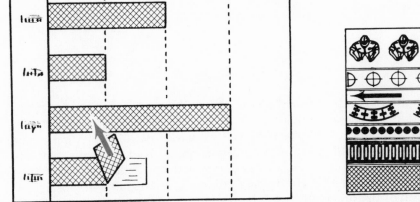

3. Revision

Sample

2. Cut the tape where desired with a stylus or knife and pull away excess tape, holding the tape at a 45° angle. Trim away excess tape at the starting point. Burnish tape firmly into place.

3. If charts are to be revised, peel off tape at a 45° angle as illustrated, to avoid tearing the chart. Apply a new strip of tape to the chart to complete the revision.

Materials Sources

Chart-Pak Inc.
Labelon Tape Co.

FLAT OPAQUE LETTERS

Teachers often have a need for flat opaque letters for use on charts, graphs, and displays of all types. Gummed-paper letters, construction-paper letters, and flexible-plastic letters are especially useful.

GUMMED-PAPER LETTERS

Gummed-paper letters, figures, and symbols are available in a large assortment of styles and sizes, ranging from $1/8''$ to $4''$ in height.

GUMMED-PAPER LETTERS

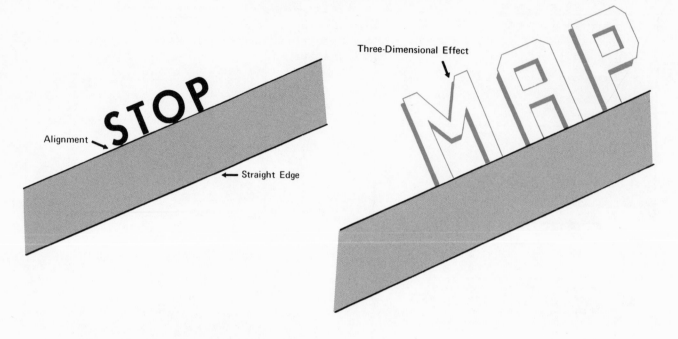

Procedure

Select the letters to be used and lay them out on the display. A straight edge, such as a ruler or T-square, may be used as a guide for even, straight placement. With a soft lead pencil, make tick marks on the display where the letters are to be placed; then, moisten the gummed back of each letter and press it into place. A pleasing three-dimensional or shadow effect may be achieved by choosing two contrasting colors of letters, superimposing one color on top of the other, slightly offset as illustrated.

Materials Source

Gummed Paper Letters: The Tablet & Ticket Co.

CONSTRUCTION-PAPER LETTERS

Paper letters cut from construction paper give quite satisfactory results when temporary, flat opaque letters are needed.

Procedure

When cutting paper letters for use on display, use a stencil, die-cut cardboard, or other commercial letters as a pattern if possible. Cut two sheets at once, contrasting colors, so a shadow effect may be achieved if desired. (*Note*: Hold the two sheets of paper together with a paper clip or spring clip while cutting as illustrated.) For a three-dimensional effect with a single letter, mount on the board with pins and pull the letter out from the board to the heads of the pins.

Materials Sources (Commercially Prepared Cardboard and Paper Letters)

Carlo's.
Hilary Co.
Redikut Letter Co.

CONSTRUCTION-PAPER LETTERS

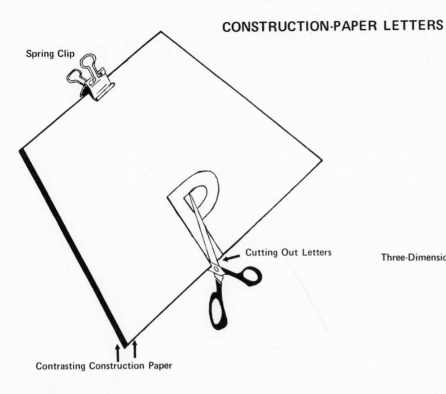

Spring Clip

Cutting Out Letters

Contrasting Construction Paper

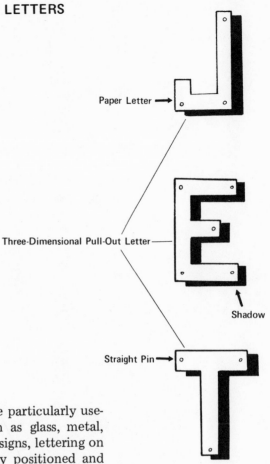

Paper Letter

Three-Dimensional Pull-Out Letter

Shadow

Straight Pin

FLEXIBLE-PLASTIC LETTERS

Large flat opaque plastic letters are available which are particularly useful for temporary lettering on any smooth surface such as glass, metal, plastic, and finished wood. These letters are used for door signs, lettering on windows, and various types of displays. They are simply positioned and pressed into place, and may be easily removed to be used again. Flexible-plastic letters can be obtained from Cling-Tite Letters, 866 N. Wabash Avenue, Chicago, Ill. 60611.

Plastice Letters

Glass Surface

FLEXIBLE-PLASTIC LETTERS

THREE-DIMENSIONAL LETTERS

The use of three-dimensional letters is an especially effective way of dramatizing bulletin-board displays. Three types of three-dimensional letters are described in this section: plaster letters, tile or plastic letters, and wood letters.

PLASTER LETTERS

Plaster-letter sets may be purchased, or easily constructed by any teacher, and are especially useful when three-dimensional letters are needed for bulletin-board displays and other instructional materials. With proper care, plaster letters will give years of useful service.

Materials and Equipment for Making Plaster Letters

casting plaster
bowl or cup
spoon for stirring plaster
Vaseline
tempera paint (powdered)
oil-base modeling clay
original 3-dimensional letter (plaster, plastic, or wood)
small nails or brads
sandpaper

Procedure

Coat the letter to be duplicated with Vaseline, and place *face up* on a flat working surface. Then:

1. Build a clay retaining wall approximately 1″ from the outer edge of the letter and 1″ higher than the letter is thick.

2. Mix the plaster until a creamy consistency is achieved; then, pour the plaster over the letter within the retaining wall.

3. Allow the plaster to harden and cool. After the plaster is cool, remove the clay retaining wall, turn the hardened plaster over, and remove the original letter from the cast. The mold is now ready to use.

4. Coat the interior of the mold with Vaseline. Mix the plaster, and pour slowly into the mold. (*Note*: Colored letters may be produced by mixing powdered tempera paint with the plaster before pouring.) Remove any bubbles that may form by stirring the plaster immediately after pouring, or by pulling bubbles off with a medicine dropper. Nails or brads to hold the plaster letters in place on a bulletin board should be inserted into the plaster head down after the plaster begins to set, or harden.

5. After the plaster has hardened and cooled, remove the duplicated letter from the mold, and sand off any rough edges. The letter is now ready to use.

To save time, a gang mold can be made to speed up the production process. Simply coat several letters with Vaseline, lay them face down on a flat working surface, build a clay retaining wall around all of them, and continue with the duplication process in much the same way as was outlined for the production of an individual letter.

Materials Sources (Commercially Prepared Plaster Letters)

Hernard Manufacturing Co.
Mitten Designer Letters.

PLASTER LETTERS

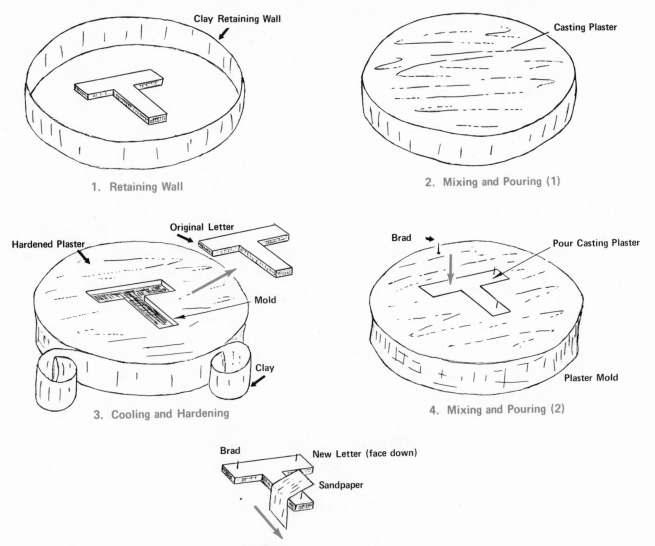

1. Retaining Wall

2. Mixing and Pouring (1)

3. Cooling and Hardening

4. Mixing and Pouring (2)

5. Sanding

TILE OR PLASTIC LETTERS

Tile or plastic letters are especially attractive when used in conjunction with bulletin-board displays, and come in an assortment of styles, sizes, and colors. Letters are available which are backed with an adhesive, or with pins in the back to help hold them firmly in place on the bulletin board. These letters are useful in photographic work for such things as labels for individual slides and titles for slide sets, and serve nicely as patterns for wood letters or cardboard letters. Letters made of tile or plastic are available from photographic-supply and school-supply houses. Plastic letters can be purchased directly from W. S. Stensgaard and Associates, 30 Rockefeller Plaza, New York, N.Y. 10020

WOOD LETTERS

Wood letters are available from several commercial concerns; however, many teachers may prefer to cut their own letters to fulfill specific lettering needs. Acceptable letters may be cut with a jig saw from scraps of plywood,

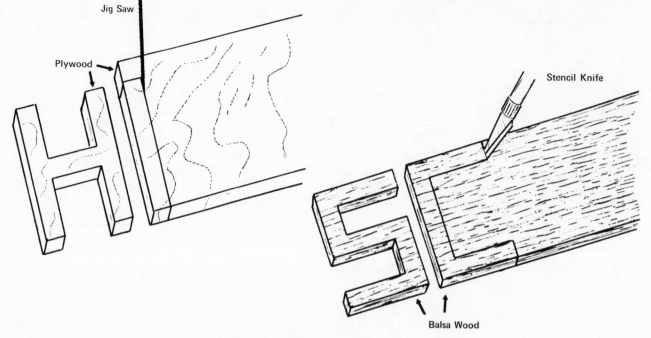

or with a razor blade or stencil knife from balsa wood. Balsa is available in sheet form from hobby shops.

Procedure

Die-cut commercially prepared paper or cardboard letters may be used as templates to aid in marking letter outlines on wood prior to cutting out the letters. After letters have been cut out, sanded, and finished, they may be fastened to a display with rubber cement, re-usable plastic, or bulletin-board wax.

Materials Sources (Commercially Prepared Wood Letters)

Manhattan Wood Letter Co.
New York Wood Letter Co.

LETTERING FOR SPECIAL EFFECTS

In addition to the more usual lettering techniques, teachers may find that certain readily available materials may be used to greatly enhance the effectiveness of a display. Materials such as cotton, sand, paper strips, colored tapes, yarn, string, paper straws, and rope can be of use to a creative teacher. The accompanying illustrations show how these materials are used to create lettering for special effects.

In addition to the special-effects lettering illustrated, teachers have found that pieces of colored chalk, broken to widths of the letters to be made, are very useful for creating soft-looking letters on construction paper, or other papers with textured surfaces. Colored paper cut to free-form shapes makes a very pleasing foundation or background for chalk lettering. To form letters, hold the chalk between the first finger and thumb, press down firmly on the paper, moving with a smooth even motion as each letter is drawn. If letters are to be used repeatedly, they may be fixed with plastic spray; teachers should be aware, however, that fixing or preserving with plastic spray will often cause color changes in construction paper.

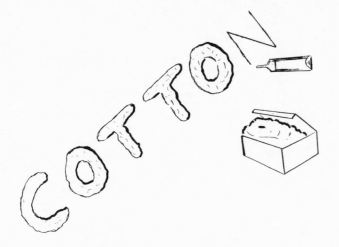

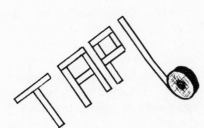

Display
and
Study Boards
and
Devices

IV

Directions for constructing several types of flannel boards, magnetic boards, combination boards, individual chalkboards, electric question boards, display easels, visographs, accordion-fold displays, and diorama stages are presented here. These devices may be used by students and teachers alike in learning centers for individual instruction. They may also be used for small-group and large-group instruction.

FLANNEL BOARDS

Flannel boards or felt boards have long been favorite tools of elementary-school teachers, and are becoming more popular with teachers on the secondary and college levels as well. Through the use of the flannel board, teachers can develop complex concepts or tell stories through easily understood step-by-step presentations. Flannel boards are both simple to construct and easy to use. Detailed directions are given for construction of a metal-hinged folding board. Illustrations are also included for construction of other types of flannel boards. In the next section are instructions for making a combination flannel and magnetic board.

METAL-HINGED FOLDING FLANNEL BOARD

Materials and Equipment

    plywood cut to size (usually 24″ × 36″; ³⁄₈″ or ¹⁄₂″ thick)
    saw
    piano hinge
    screwdriver
    screws
    flannel or felt cut to the desired size (30″ × 42″ for a 24″ × 36″ board)
    stapler and staples
    hammer
    roll of masking or plastic tape
    pencil

To construct a durable folding flannel board:

1. Cut the plywood into two halves. Place the boards face up on a table and mark with a pencil the placement of the hinge on both halves of the mounting board using the hinge as a guide for marking. Remove the hinge and cut a depression in the plywood deep enough to allow for flush mounting of the hinge. Fit the halves of the board snugly together and mount the hinge flush with the surface of the board as illustrated.

2. Lay the flannel or felt *nap side down* on a smooth surface. Place the plywood on top of the cloth with the hinged side against the material. Fold an edge of the flannel over onto the back of the board and staple it down. Next, turn the board over and smooth the flannel tight across the face of the board.

3. Holding the flannel snug, press the board, flannel side down, onto the work surface and staple the other three edges of the flannel into place.

4. Cover the stapled edges (on the back of the flannel board) with strips of masking or plastic tape. Carefully cut the flannel and the tape at the joint

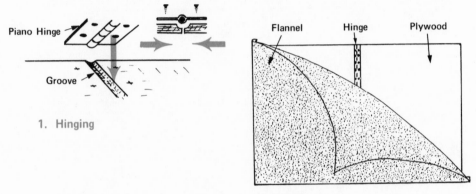

Piano Hinge

Groove

1. Hinging

Flannel   Hinge   Plywood

2. Covering

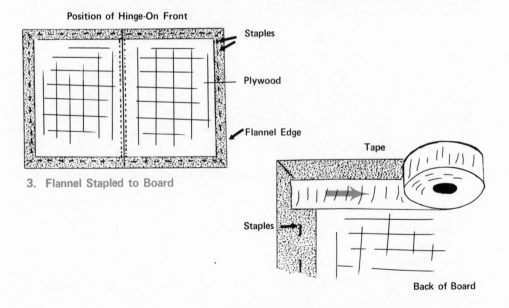

Position of Hinge-On Front

Staples

Plywood

Flannel Edge

3. Flannel Stapled to Board

Tape

Staples

Back of Board

4. Taping to Cover Staples

METAL-HINGED FOLDING FLANNEL BOARD

on each edge so that the board will fold with the flannel-covered sides inside. Straps or handles may be added at the ends of the board for ease in carrying. The board is now ready to use. (*Note*: When using the board, be sure to slant it slightly, so materials used will adhere more readily to the surface.)

SLIP-COVER FLANNEL BOARD

Cut the board to size. Cut the flannel so that two pieces are 1″ wider on all sides than the dimensions of the cardboard (or plywood). Sew three sides, slip over the cardboard, and stitch closed.

FOLDING CARDBOARD FLANNEL BOARD

Cut four pieces of heavyweight cardboard to equal dimensions. Tape as illustrated, and cover the two center pieces with flocked adhesive shelf paper. Assemble and tape together, overlapping the two end pieces as shown in the drawing.

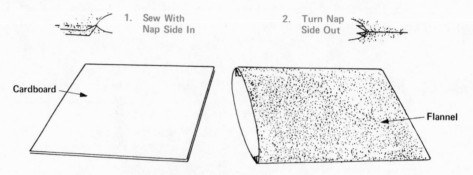

SLIP-COVER FLANNEL BOARD

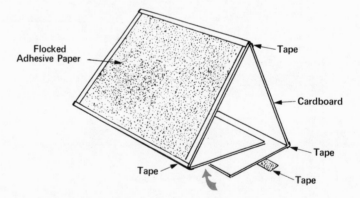

FOLDING CARDBOARD FLANNEL BOARD

Materials Sources for Flannel Boards

Instructo Products.
The Judy Company
The Ohio Flock-Cote Company
Oravisual Company, Inc.
Techni-Craft.

Instructional Materials That Can Be Used on the Flannel Board

1. Figures or letters cut out of flannel or felt.

2. Pictures cut from books or magazines and backed with flannel, felt, corduroy, or lightweight sandpaper. Use rubber cement or fast-drying glue to fasten the adhering material to the back of the picture.

3. Small, lightweight pictures printed on textured paper. These often need no backing to keep them on the flannel board.

4. Pictures backed with flocking. Flocking, available in cans, is very easy and convenient to use.

5. Pictures backed with flocked adhesive shelf paper.

6. String or yarn will adhere to the board without backing.

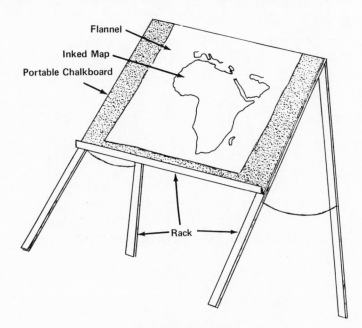

FLANNEL MAP

FLANNEL MAP

Teachers specializing in the social-studies area may wish to construct a flannel board, and draw the outline of a map directly on the flannel-board surface with India ink, quick-drying paint, or a felt-tipped pen (page 62). However, a satisfactory folding flannel map may be made by drawing a map outline on a piece of unmounted flannel. To use a flannel map of this type, drape the cloth over a chalkboard or bulletin board and fasten at the top with a strip of pressure-sensitive tape, or place over a flannel board and smooth into place. As the map is used, symbols may be added to the outline map to give detail in the presentation. After the lesson is completed, the map should be pulled loose and stored in a folder or an envelope along with the symbols used.

MAGNETIC BOARDS

A magnetic chalkboard is an extremely versatile device and lends itself especially well to presentations which require repeated use of accurate symbolic representation, or accuracy in scale and form (such as geometric shapes and electrical-circuit symbols). The magnetic chalkboard is also useful for storytelling, coaching, and almost any lesson presentation which requires movement and progression in presentation. Cardboard cutouts glued to small magnets will readily adhere to the steel surface of the board; lightweight pictures may be held in place on the board by magnets placed at the corners.

Materials held in place by magnetic attraction may be easily supplemented by materials drawn on the board with chalk. Many teachers have found the magnetic chalkboard to be an invaluable addition to their supply of teaching tools.

Detailed directions are given for making (1) a framed magnetic chalk-board, and (2) a cookie-sheet magnetic board.

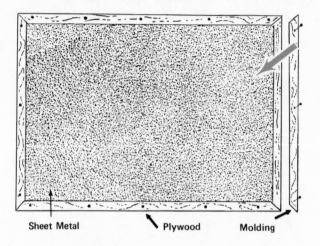

Sheet Metal   Plywood   Molding

FRAMED MAGNETIC CHALKBOARD

FRAMED MAGNETIC CHALKBOARD

Materials and Equipment

$\frac{1}{4}$" plywood (usually 24" × 36")
sheet iron or sheet steel (common "sheet tin" works nicely). 2" less in length and width than the plywood
glue or adhesive that will hold metal to wood
1" molding—enough to frame the steel
small brads or nails
small magnets
paint brush
chalkboard paint

Procedure

Secure all the needed materials and equipment. Then:

1. Paint the sheet iron or steel with chalkboard paint. If galvanized metal is used, the surface of the metal must first be chemically treated, or cleaned. Coat the surface of the galvanized sheet with common household vinegar, and allow to stand for 15 minutes; then wash the sheet with tap water. As soon as the metal dries, it is ready for the application of chalkboard paint or automobile enamel. A minimum of *two coats* of paint should be applied, carefully following the manufacturer's directions.

2. When the paint dries glue the iron or steel to the plywood base, chalkboard (painted) side up, leaving a 1" border on all sides.

3. Cut the 1" molding to frame the iron on all sides and glue or nail the molding to the plywood backing. Finish the molding with paint or varnish if desired.

A steel cookie sheet may be used as a magnetic chalkboard after black adhesive shelf paper has been applied.

Materials and Equipment

cookie sheet (steel—aluminum won't work)
black adhesive shelf paper ("Con-Tact" or other)
long ruler
scissors

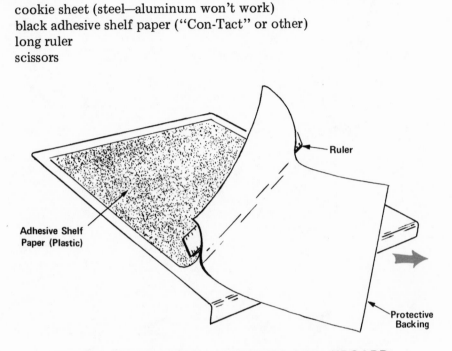

Ruler

Adhesive Shelf
Paper (Plastic)

Protective
Backing

STEEL COOKIE-SHEET MAGNETIC CHALKBOARD

Procedure

Clean the cookie sheet *thoroughly* with hand soap or detergent. Allow it to dry. Apply the black adhesive shelf paper, which is cut smaller than the cookie-sheet dimensions. First, start removing the paper backing at one corner only. Stick the shelf paper (black plastic) down to the cookie sheet. Pull the backing sheet *out from under* the shelf paper, following the separation line with a ruler to ensure even, complete adhesion to the metal surface. Leave a border of metal showing around the edges.

To make the plastic surface ready to take chalk marks, coat it with chalk dust from a chalkboard eraser—rub the dusty eraser firmly over the black surface.

The magnetic chalkboard is now ready to use.

COMBINATION MAGNETIC BOARD AND FLANNEL BOARD

A combination board is easy to construct, and gives teachers and students options otherwise unavailable. The board may be quickly and easily constructed using readily available materials at little cost.

Materials and Equipment

galvanized steel oil-drip pan (available from auto-supply stores, hardware stores)
flocked adhesive shelf paper (from hardware store), or flannel and white glue

COMBINATION MAGNETIC BOARD AND FLANNEL BOARD

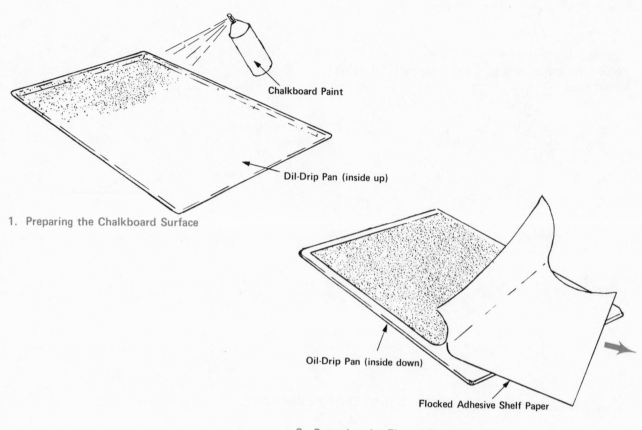

Chalkboard Paint

Dil-Drip Pan (inside up)

1. Preparing the Chalkboard Surface

Oil-Drip Pan (inside down)

Flocked Adhesive Shelf Paper

2. Preparing the Flannel-Board Surface

vinegar
chalkboard paint (aerosol or brush-applied)
scissors

Procedure

1. Clean the inside of the drip pan with vinegar and water. Allow it to dry thoroughly, and apply chalkboard paint according to the directions on the can. After the chalkboard surface is dry, pat it and rub it with a chalk-dust-filled eraser.

2. Turn the pan over and apply adhesive shelf paper as illustrated. (For details, see the directions for applying shelf paper as described on page 93 for the *steel cookie-sheet magnetic board*.) If you use flannel instead of the flocked paper, cut the flannel to size, mark the pan area to be covered, and spread glue on it. Roll the flannel onto the glue as soon as it becomes tacky, using a ruler to prevent wrinkles. The combination board is now ready to use.

PREPARING MATERIALS FOR USE WITH MAGNETIC BOARDS

Construction paper, tagboard, cardboard—all may be used in preparing symbols for use on the magnetic board. Draw the symbols and cut them out, then tape or glue magnets to their backs. Small real objects may be prepared and displayed in the same way. Taped magnets may be removed easily for

MATERIALS FOR USE WITH MAGNETIC BOARDS

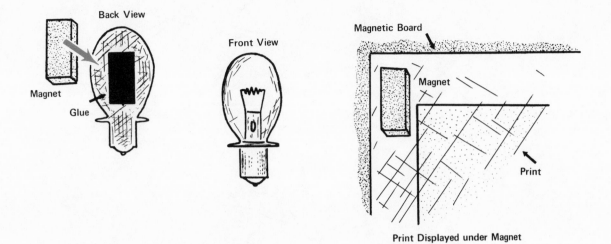

Print Displayed under Magnet

use on other symbols. Plastic magnetic strips are especially easy to use, are self-adhesive, and may be easily cut to size with a pair of scissors. Pictures and other graphics may be displayed on the surface of the board by placing magnets on the picture corners, as illustrated.

Materials Sources

Mach-A-Tach.
Maggie Magnetic, Inc.
Magnet Sales Co.
Multi-Plastics Co.
Program Aids Co., Inc.
Ronald Eyrich.

INDIVIDUAL CHALKBOARDS

Teachers may prepare individual chalkboards for children to use at their desks or in learning centers. These can be made at little cost, using readily available materials.

Materials and Equipment

For painted chalkboard:
    masonite or plywood
    saw
    chalkboard paint (brush or aerosol type)
    shellac or varnish
    brush
    brush cleaner or turpentine
For cardboard chalkboard with black adhesive shelf-paper surface:
    heavy-weight, pressed cardboard
    black adhesive shelf paper ("Con-Tact" or other)
    ruler
    scissors
    paper cutter

INDIVIDUAL CHALKBOARDS

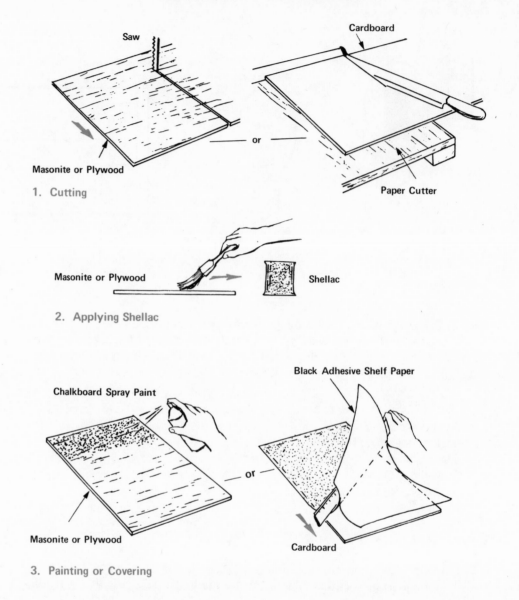

1. Cutting

2. Applying Shellac

3. Painting or Covering

Procedure—Painted Chalkboard

1. Cut wood or masonite to size (usually 8″ × 10″ or 11″ × 14″).
2. Prepare the surface for paint by coating it with shellac. Allow the shellac to dry completely before proceeding.
3. Paint the surface with chalkboard paint. Chalkboard paint is available for use in cans for brush application or in aerosol spray cans. Two coats of paint are needed. Follow the manufacturer's directions. When the paint is thoroughly dry, prepare the surface to take chalk by rubbing with a chalk-filled eraser. The board is now ready to use.

Procedure—Cardboard Chalkboard

1. Cut the cardboard to size (usually 8″ × 10″ or 11″ × 14″).
2. If the cardboard is smooth-surfaced, no shellac is needed. If in doubt, apply shellac and allow it to dry.

3. Cover the cardboard surface with black adhesive shelf paper, using the procedure described for the steel cookie-sheet magnetic chalkboard (page 93).

ELECTRIC QUESTION BOARDS

The electric question board, a simple teaching machine, may be constructed easily by classroom teachers or by older students. This device will provide many hours of useful and interesting individual instruction. The electric question board may be used in any subject area where knowledge of related facts is deemed desirable and necessary. Many teachers make excellent use of electric question boards in learning centers.

When using the electric question board the student touches the end of the wire or line on the *left*-hand side of the board to a question terminal (bolt or foil next to the question) and the answer wire or line on the *right*-hand side of the board to an answer terminal (bolt or foil). A bulb will light up when the correct choice has been selected.

WOODEN MATCHING ELECTRIC QUESTION BOARD

Materials and Equipment

> one piece of wood, 1″ soft pine or ¼″ to ½″ plywood, 18″ × 24″
> one piece of wood 4″ to 6″ wide, 24″ long
> brace and bits or hand drill electric drill with assorted sizes of wood bits
> low-voltage bulb, battery, battery bracket, socket
> saw
> several feet of insulated wire (bell wire or other single-conductor wire)
> 16 stove bolts with nuts and washers
> household cement or other permanent waterproof glue
> tagboard or other pliable, light cardboard
> scissors
> finishing nails and hammer
> pencil and yardstick or ruler
> staples

Procedure

Cut the wooden top to 18″ × 24″. Then:

1. Draw a diagonal line from one lower corner of the 4″ × 24″ board to the opposite upper corner and saw along this line. The two triangular-shaped halves will serve as the sides of the electric question board.

2. Nail the top to the sides as illustrated. Draw vertical lines from the top to the bottom of the board face, approximately 4″ from each side. Draw 8 short *horizontal* lines spaced every 2⅝″ along both *vertical* lines to serve as drill references. Drill holes, 8 on each side, for stove bolts; then drill a hole in the *center* of the board for the low-voltage bulb.

3. Fasten the stove bolts in place, with the washers and nuts together on the *underside* of the board. Fashion question and answer holders as illustrated from tagboard or light cardboard and glue into place beside the stove bolts. Fasten the lamp socket into the hole provided and screw the low-voltage bulb into place.

4. Wire the underside of the box, connecting an *answer* terminal (bolt) to a *question* terminal (bolt) for each pair of questions and answers (eight pairs in all). Fasten the battery bracket to one side of the box on the inside and connect a wire from one end of the battery bracket to the bulb socket.

WOODEN MATCHING ELECTRIC QUESTION BOARD

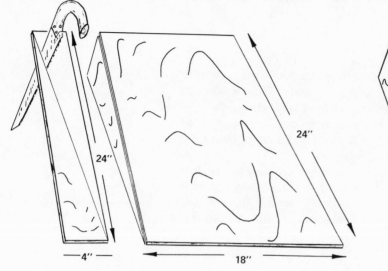

24″   24″   24″

4″   18″

1. Assembling Board

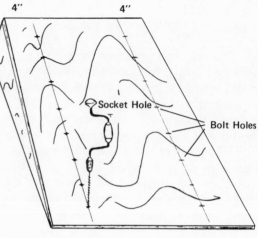

4″   4″

Socket Hole

Bolt Holes

2. Drilling

Light Bulb

Socket

Bolt

¼″   1″

2″

Question Holder   Answer Holder

Fold   Fold

3. Fastening

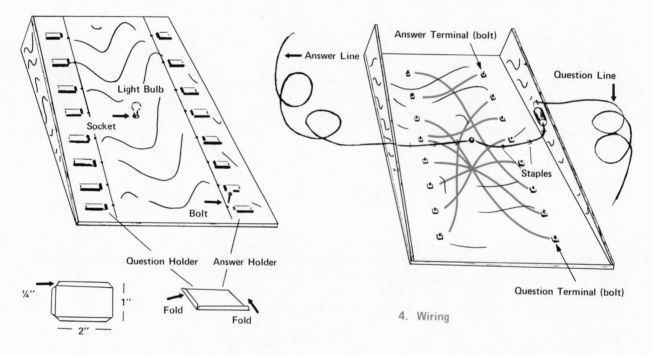

Answer Terminal (bolt)

Answer Line

Question Line

Staples

Question Terminal (bolt)

4. Wiring

A connecting *answer line* should go from the bulb socket to the outside of the box. Be sure to allow enough line to reach all the answers provided on the face of the board. The *question line* should extend to the outside of the box from the battery and be long enough to reach all the questions.

The electric question board is now ready for operation. Whenever a correct answer is matched with a question by touching the answer line to an answer terminal-bolt and the question line to the proper question terminal-bolt the bulb lights up confirming the correct response.

To keep children from memorizing the location of matching terminals, occasionally rewire the connections from answer terminals to question terminals and change the placement of questions and answers accordingly.

ELECTRIC QUESTION BOARD MADE WITH CARDBOARD AND KITCHEN FOIL

To construct an electric question board with cardboard and kitchen foil is easy and inexpensive since these materials are readily available. Pupils as young as grade 5 can make these and can use them for getting across useful and interesting information to their classmates.

Materials and Equipment

paper
aluminum foil
rubber cement
paper cutter or scissors
cardboard or manila folder
tape
hole puncher
transparent plastic sheet or plastic bag
battery and matching lamp bulb
bell wire
1 brad
pencil
ruler

Procedure

1. Cement the foil to the paper, using rubber cement.
2. Cut the paper-backed foil into strips. Cut the cardboard to the desired size; two pieces the *same size* will be needed.
3. Punch holes in *one* sheet of cardboard as illustrated. Tape the cardboard pieces together at *one edge only*. Draw lines from *question holes* to *answer holes* using a pencil and ruler. Tape the foil strips to the board, *foil side down*, with each end of a strip covering a hole as shown, until all the circuit lines have been covered.
4. Fold the cardboard pieces together and close the open edge with tape. Attach a transparent plastic bag or sheet of plastic to the board with tape as shown.
5. Construct an answer indicator as shown. A bracket, if available, is better than tape for holding the battery and bulb in place; hardware and radio stores often sell such brackets at little cost. Attach wires as shown, taking care to remove insulation at both ends. Tape the answer indicator to a piece of cardboard, as shown. An additional piece of cardboard is used as a cover.
6. Glue the answer indicator to the circuit board. Fold the cover of the indicator closed so only the bulb shows; fasten it down with a brad. The board is ready to use, as soon as questions and answers, matching the circuitry, are printed or typed on a piece of paper and put behind the plastic sheet or into the plastic bag.

When one touches the foil to the left of a question with the question wire and at the same time touches the foil to the right of the correct answer with the answer wire the bulb will light up, indicating that the answer selected is the correct choice.

ELECTRIC QUESTION BOARD-CARDBOARD AND FOIL

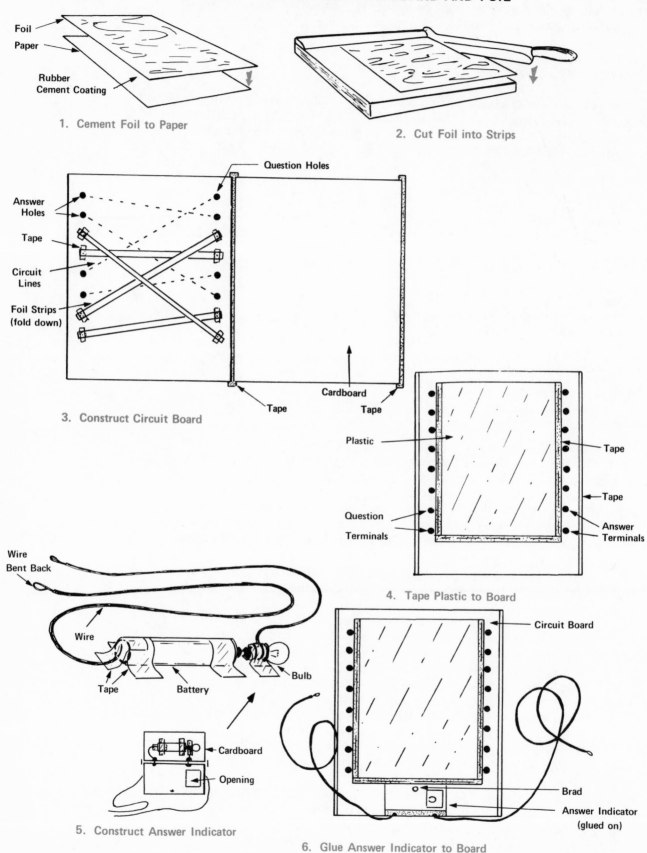

Foil

Paper

Rubber
Cement Coating

1. Cement Foil to Paper

2. Cut Foil into Strips

Question Holes

Answer
Holes

Tape

Circuit
Lines

Foil Strips
(fold down)

Cardboard

Tape

Tape

3. Construct Circuit Board

Plastic

Question
Terminals

Tape

Tape

Answer
Terminals

4. Tape Plastic to Board

Wire
Bent Back

Wire

Tape   Battery

Bulb

Cardboard

Opening

5. Construct Answer Indicator

Circuit Board

Brad

Answer Indicator
(glued on)

6. Glue Answer Indicator to Board

MULTIPLE-CHOICE ELECTRIC QUESTION BOARD

Materials and Equipment

cardboard or masonite, cut to desired size
strips of wood, for frame
scissors to punch hole in cardboard, or drill for making holes in masonite
glue, to fasten cardboard to wood frame
low-voltage bulb and socket
several feet of insulated wire (bell wire or other single-conductor wire)
20 steel stove bolts with nuts and washers
clear acetate or plastic
cloth tape or transparent tape
battery bracket, screws
screwdriver

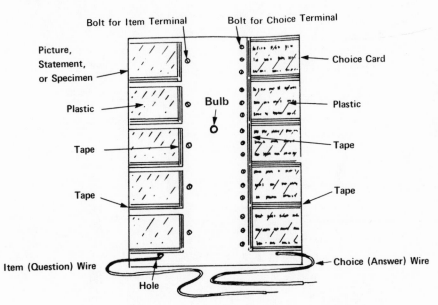

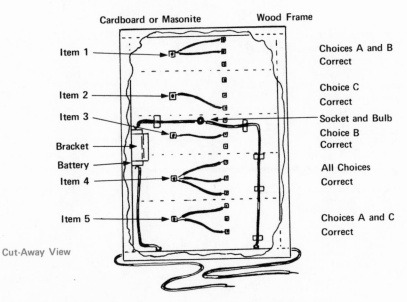

Cut-Away View

MULTIPLE-CHOICE ELECTRIC QUESTION BOARD

1. Cut the board to the desired size. Cut the wood strips to make a frame. Glue the wood strips to the board around the edges, as illustrated.

2. Mark off the positions of the plastic item and choice holders. Mark the positions of the bolt terminal holes for items and answer choices.

3. Tape the plastic on the cardboard as illustrated. Drill or punch holes for the bolts. Push the bolts through the holes. Invert the board, and wire as illustrated. Be sure to remove the insulation from the *ends* of the wires.

4. Attach battery bracket, using screws or nails.

5. Tape or staple the question and answer wires into place. Make holes for them and push them through their respective holes, as illustrated.

6. Insert item cards, specimens, or pictures, and answer-choice cards. The board is now ready to use.

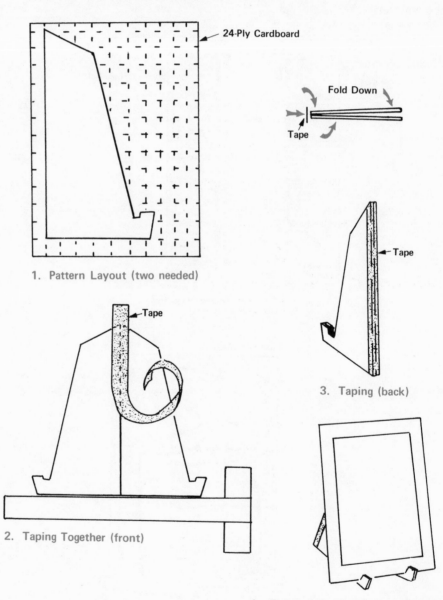

1. Pattern Layout (two needed)

Fold Down

Tape

3. Taping (back)

Tape

2. Taping Together (front)

4. Finished Easel with Mounted Material

DISPLAY EASEL

When an *item bolt* and a *choice bolt* which are wired together are touched by the *item* wire and the *choice* wire the circuit is completed, causing the bulb to light up. By the way the item bolts and answer bolts are connected, one may have any of *all* choices apply, either of *two* choices, or any *one* choice. Pictures, specimens, or written materials may be placed on the item side; choices may be arranged to teach basic facts about the items displayed, or to help the student know whether his deductions are correct.

DISPLAY EASEL

A display easel for mounted materials is easy to make, and quite useful when preparing a display. The display may be variously used: to attract attention, for motivation, in interest or learning centers.

Materials and Equipment

> 24-ply cardboard
> pencil
> pressure-sensitive tape
> straight edge (ruler or T-square)
> knife or other cutting instrument

Procedure

1. Refer to the pattern layout in the illustration to determine the proportions for the display easel halves. The size of the easel should be determined by the dimensions of the mounted materials to be displayed. Measure and draw one side of the easel on 24-ply cardboard as illustrated. Cut this side out, lay it on a second piece of cardboard, and trace the outline with a pencil. Cut out the second half.

2. Join the two pieces together with tape as shown, using a straight edge (T-square) to line up the bottom edges of the cardboard pieces.

3. Fold the two pieces with the *tape inside* and apply tape to the *back* of the easel as shown. This double taping helps to give rigidity and strength to the device.

4. Display materials on the easel as shown.

Some teachers decorate easels they have made with patterned shelf paper, or spray them with acrylic paints.

VISOGRAPH

A visograph is a transparent-faced display pocket with one open edge. It is very useful for displaying unmounted pictures under a protective plastic covering. In addition, a visograph may be used as an erasable holding device for work sheets, tests, and outline maps, since one may write or draw on the plastic surface with grease (wax) pencil or water-soluble felt pens and then erase quickly and easily without damage to the instructional materials. Creative teachers will find many uses for the visograph in learning centers and for other applications as well.

Material and Equipment

> plastic or acetate (.005″ gauge or thicker is most desirable)
> cardboard
> pressure-sensitive tape (cloth is very attractive)
> scissors
> razor blade or knife
> metal-edged ruler

VISOGRAPH

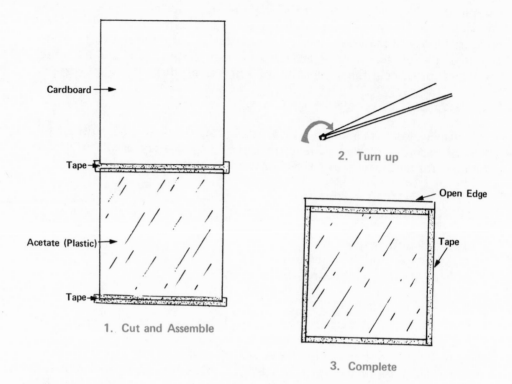

1. Cut and Assemble

2. Turn up

3. Complete

Procedure

1. Cut the cardboard base to the desired dimensions (according to the size of materials to be inserted into the visograph). A base 11" × 14" will accommodate most pictures and worksheets. Cut the plastic to the same *width*, but slightly *shorter length*. Cut three pieces of tape longer than the width of the cardboard. Apply one piece to the *back bottom edge* of the cardboard, allowing the tape to *overlap* by half its width. Turn the cardboard over, and place the plastic (acetate) sheet on the sticky tape as illustrated, leaving a separation between board and plastic of about ⅛". Add a second piece of tape over *the top of the first piece* of tape; trim off the excess tape at the ends. Add a third piece of tape at the opposite edge of the plastic sheet and fold over; trim off excess tape.

2. Fold the plastic sheet up and onto the cardboard.

3. Tape along both sides.

The visograph is now ready for use.

VISOGRAPH ACCORDION FOLD

A visograph accordion fold is very useful for displaying pictures in sequence or for giving directions for completing a particular assignment or procedure. The fold most commonly is used standing on a table as illustrated.

Materials and Equipment

several completed visographs (see directions, immediately preceding)
pressure-sensitive tape
scissors

VISOGRAPH ACCORDION FOLD

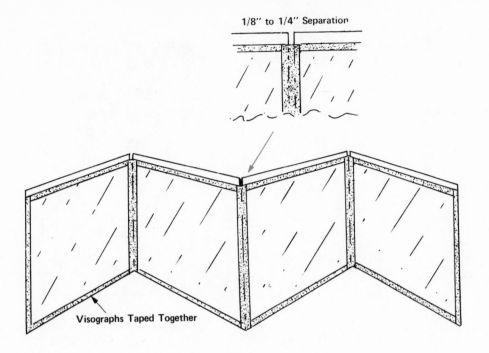

1/8" to 1/4" Separation

Visographs Taped Together

Procedure

Place the visographs *face up* on the table. Separate them from ¹/₈" to ¹/₄", as illustrated. Use a yardstick or T-square to align the bottom edges of the visographs. Apply tape to hold sections together. Turn the assembly over; then apply strips of tape on the back side of each fold. The visograph accordion fold is now ready to use.

DIORAMA STAGES

Dioramas are effective, easy-to-construct displays useful in a number of subject areas, including language arts, social studies, and the sciences. Through the use of the diorama, teachers are often able to communicate ideas more effectively by placing objects in realistic, three-dimensional surroundings. Several types of diorama stages are illustrated, and one stage, the semicircular stage, is discussed and illustrated in a step-by-step presentation on the following pages.

Materials and Equipment—Semicircular Stage

box for use as a stage (size and type of box used will vary according to the size and style of the proposed display)

paints or felt-tipped pens for applying background (felt pens are especially easy to use on most paper or cardboard surfaces)

scissors or other cutting devices as needed for individual projects

objects for display (may be plastic models, plaster-of-Paris models, papier-mâché figures, realia such as small specimens, cardboard cutouts, or other objects)

construction paper or tagboard for use in construction of the interior of the box and as a base for background scene

DIORAMA STAGES

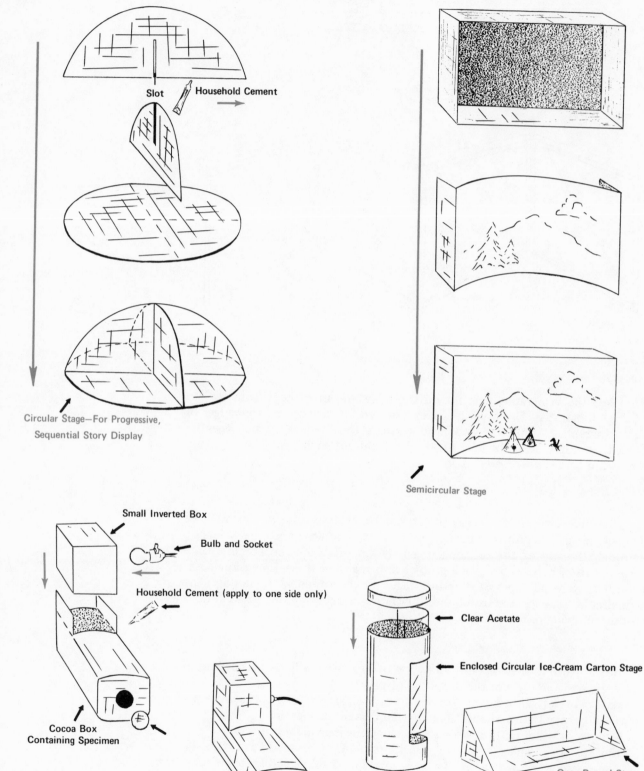

Slot

Household Cement

Circular Stage—For Progressive,
Sequential Story Display

Semicircular Stage

Small Inverted Box

Bulb and Socket

Household Cement (apply to one side only)

Clear Acetate

Enclosed Circular Ice-Cream Carton Stage

Cocoa Box
Containing Specimen

Open-Braced Stage

Lighted "Surprise" Box

DIORAMA STAGES

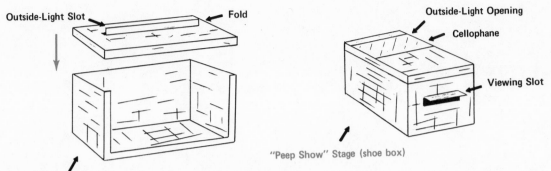

Outside-Light Slot   Fold

Enclosed Shoe-Box Stage

Outside-Light Opening
Cellophane
Viewing Slot

"Peep Show" Stage (shoe box)

extension cord with socket and lamp if display is to be lighted
mirror to simulate water (for a pond, pool, or lake), if needed
rubber cement or paper glue
stapler and staples
miscellaneous materials to add realism, such as rocks or twigs
pencil
sheet of paper

Procedure—Semicircular Stage

Secure all the needed materials. Then:

1. Sketch the layout on a sheet of paper. Select a box of the appropriate size and remove one side or the top

2. Measure off a piece of tagboard and fold as illustrated. Lay the tagboard flat and sketch in the desired background material. Refold the tagboard, apply rubber cement to the folded edges, and fasten into place. Use staples if desired.

3. Add display materials and label the display.

Maps,
Models,
and
Mock-Ups
V

Teacher- and student-made special-purpose maps, models, and mock-ups are very useful for motivating students and explaining specific concepts or generalizations. Selected examples of materials useful in the social sciences, natural sciences, aerospace study, and geometry are included in this section.

MAPS

Several types of maps can be constructed by teachers and students to help facilitate learning and understanding in the social-studies area. Maps found to be useful for teachers on all levels include the plastic-surfaced map and three-dimensional maps of various kinds.

PLASTIC-SURFACED MAP

A plastic-surfaced map is most useful when there is a need for the addition of details to a map during a presentation, or for checking student understanding. The map surface can be written on with a wax crayon or china-marking pencil, and later quickly and easily erased with a soft cloth; corrections can easily be made during the presentation if necessary.

Procedure

To construct a plastic-surfaced map, first select the map to be used for instructional purposes, and mount it on poster board (or other mounting board). For mounting the map, the permanent rubber-cement method (page 34) or the dry mount method (page 36) should be considered. If an outline map is needed, consider tracing a map projected from a book or slide (page 166) directly onto poster board in lieu of using a mounted map. Cut a sheet of clear acetate (plastic) the size of the poster board with the map on it, and lay on a flat surface. Cut four strips of pressure-sensitive tape the length of each edge of the acetate sheet, and attach along each edge, allowing half of the width of each strip of tape to protrude beyond the edge of the acetate on all sides. Turn the acetate sheet over so the sticky side of the tape

PLASTIC-SURFACED MAP

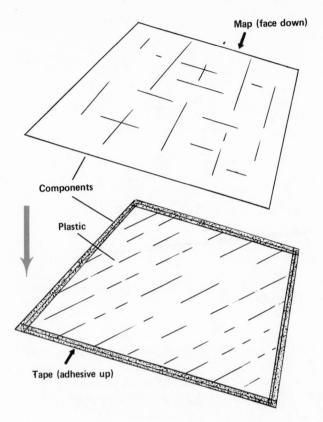

Map (face down)

Components

Plastic

Tape (adhesive up)

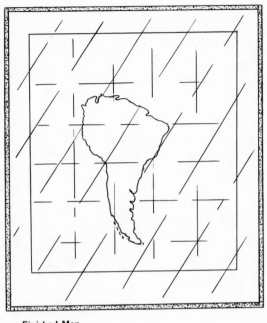

Finished Map

is up, and lay the poster board, with the map face down, on the acetate sheet. Fold the tape over onto the back of the poster board, and press into place. The plastic-surfaced map is now ready to use.

Materials Sources

Clear Acetate: Arthur Brown & Bro., Inc.
Lewis Artist Supply Co.
Major Services.

Craftint Manufacturing Co.
Transilwrap Co., Inc.

THREE-DIMENSIONAL MAP

Construction and use of three-dimensional maps may be a very worthwhile educational experience. Papier-mâché, asbestos, salt and flour, and sawdust may be used to produce effective maps for teaching and learning situations.

General Procedures

Outline the map on heavy cardboard or light plywood. Apply molding material, prepared as indicated in each instance below. After the shaping and molding of the map is complete, allow the map to dry completely, and paint as desired. The map surface may be protected by a coating of plastic spray. (*Note*: The corners of the base should be weighed down as the map dries to prevent warping.)

Papier-Mâché

Papier-mâché maps are made from paper strips (newspaper or paper toweling) soaked in a smooth, creamy wheat-paste mixture. Apply paper

THREE-DIMENSIONAL MAP

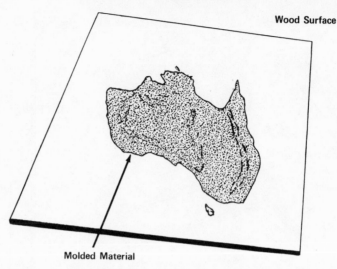

strips and mold into shape as the strips are applied. Use large, crumpled strips of paper for mountain formations.

Asbestos

Asbestos maps are made from a mixture of powdered asbestos (available from plumbing and hardware stores) and wheat paste. Add ½ cup of wheat paste to 1 pound of asbestos, and mix with water until a claylike consistency is achieved. Apply the mix to the outline map, and mold into shape.

Salt and Flour

Salt-and-flour maps are made from a mixture of equal parts of salt and flour moistened with water. Mold into shape as desired.

Sawdust

Sawdust, available from lumber yards, is an excellent medium to use in making three-dimensional maps. (*Note*: Do not use redwood or cedar sawdust.) To prepare the mixture, add wheat paste to the sawdust, and moisten until easy to mold.

PAPER FLYING MODEL AIRCRAFT

By following the illustrations and using the patterns presented here, teachers may motivate students working on an aerospace unit to make and fly their own models. To expedite their use the patterns are presented full size. To use, prepare a thermal "ditto" master from the page of this manual, using the thermal copier (Thermo-Fax) or Masterfax machine and special thermal masters (page 13) or trace the diagram onto a conventional master. Run off the copies needed, using a spirit duplicator.

Materials and Equipment

ledger paper, or other heavyweight paper—available from art- or business-supply houses
scissors
paper clip
felt- or nylon-tip pen
pencil

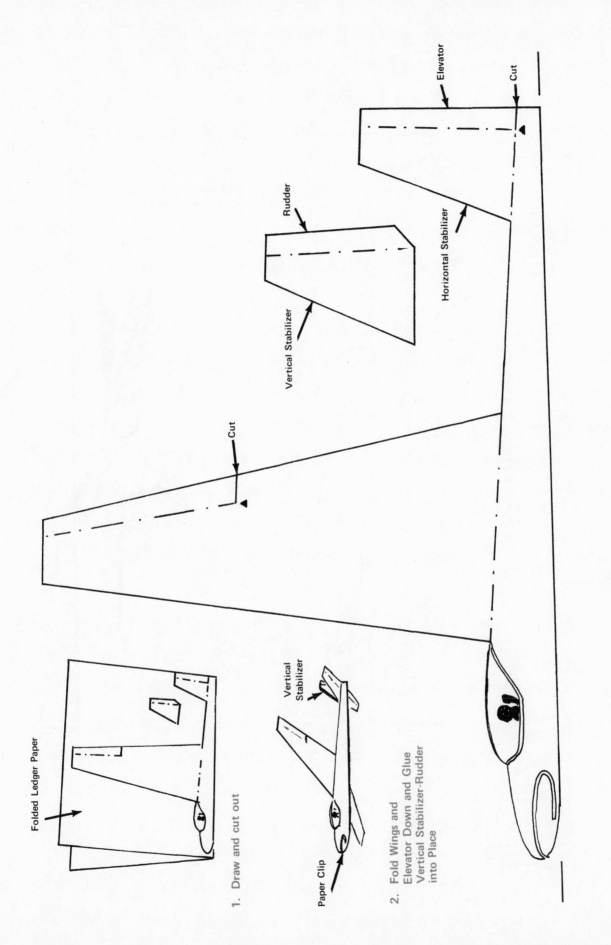

Folded Ledger Paper

1. Draw and cut out

Vertical Stabilizer

Paper Clip

2. Fold Wings and
   Elevator Down and Glue
   Vertical Stabilizer-Rudder
   into Place

Elevator

Cut

Rudder

Horizontal Stabilizer

Vertical Stabilizer

Cut

CONVENTIONAL AIRCRAFT – PATTERN

"TAIL-FIRST" AIRCRAFT

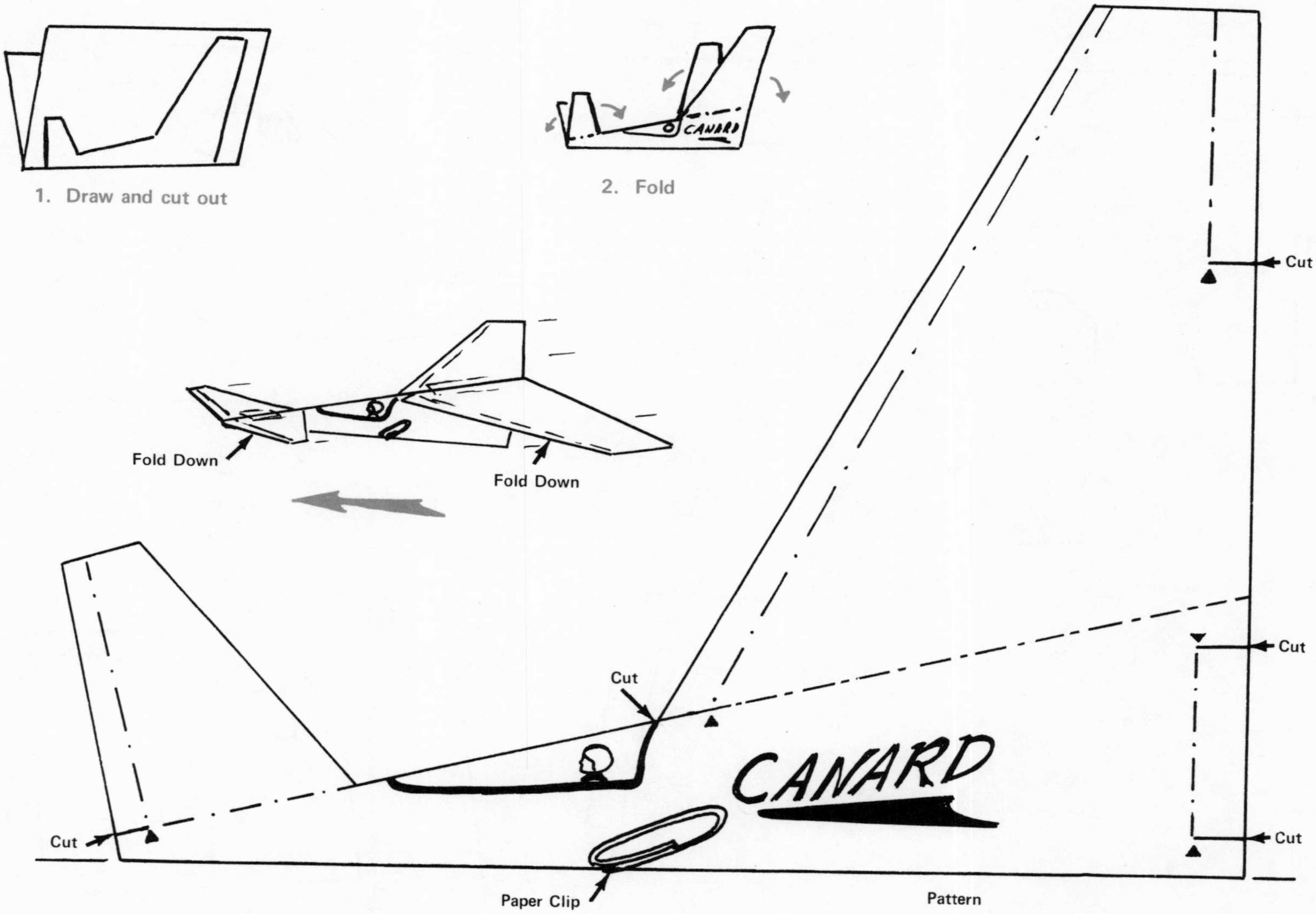

1. Draw and cut out

2. Fold

CANARD

Fold Down

Fold Down

Cut

Cut

Cut

Cut

Cut

Pattern

Paper Clip

CANARD

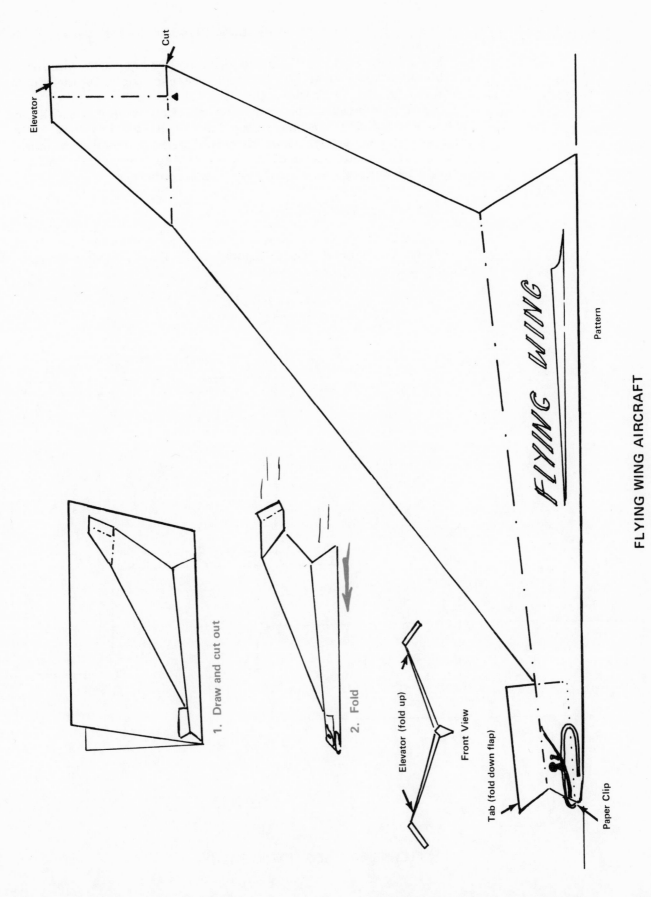

Cut

Elevator

FLYING WING

Pattern

1. Draw and cut out

2. Fold

Elevator (fold up)

Front View

Tab (fold down flap)

Paper Clip

FLYING WING AIRCRAFT

Procedure

1. Fold the ledger paper as illustrated. Trace or draw the pattern on the paper. Cut out.

2. Fold each model as illustrated. Glue the two body sides together, or use transparent tape if preferred. Add a paper-clip weight. On the *conventional* glider, remember to glue in the vertical stabilizer.

Test fly the model, adjusting the position of the paper clip until a good glide is achieved. Throw *gently*. By bending the elevators or the rudder the craft can be made to dive, climb, or turn, illustrating the effect of moving control surfaces. Students should be encouraged to design and fly their own models after working with these models to gain confidence.

MODELS OF GEOMETRIC SOLIDS

Models of geometric solids may be easily made by teachers or children and are especially useful in mathematics inquiry. Both transparent and cardboard models may be constructed.

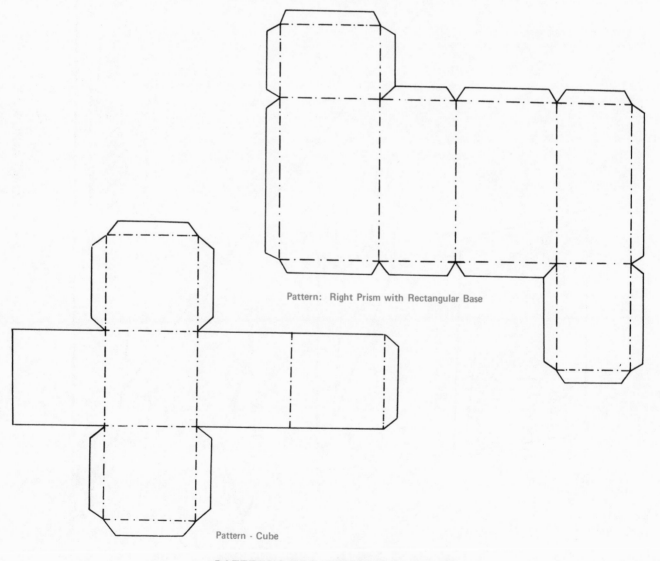

Pattern: Right Prism with Rectangular Base

Pattern - Cube

PATTERNS FOR GEOMETRIC SOLIDS

PATTERNS FOR GEOMETRIC SOLIDS

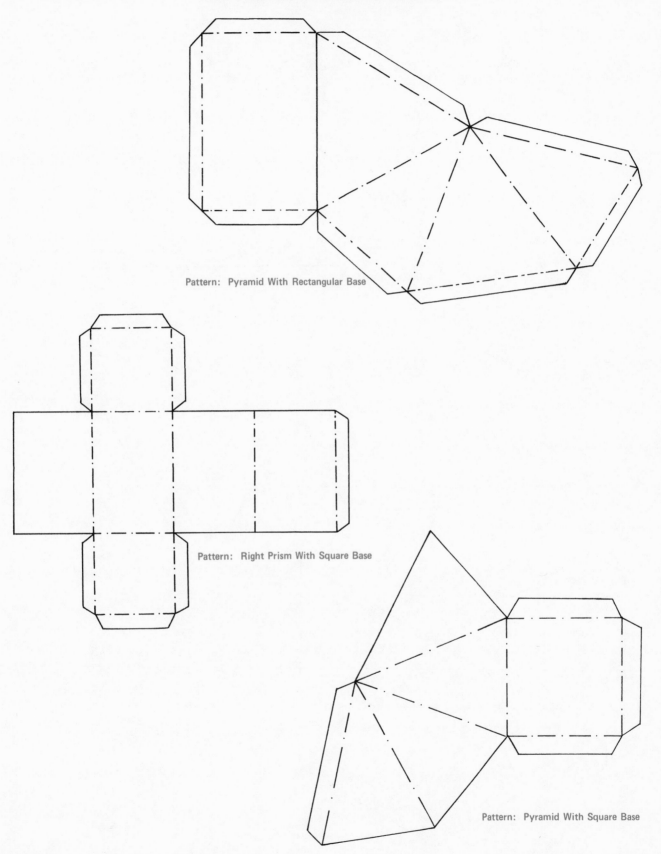

Pattern: Pyramid With Rectangular Base

Pattern: Right Prism With Square Base

Pattern: Pyramid With Square Base

PATTERNS FOR GEOMETRIC SOLIDS

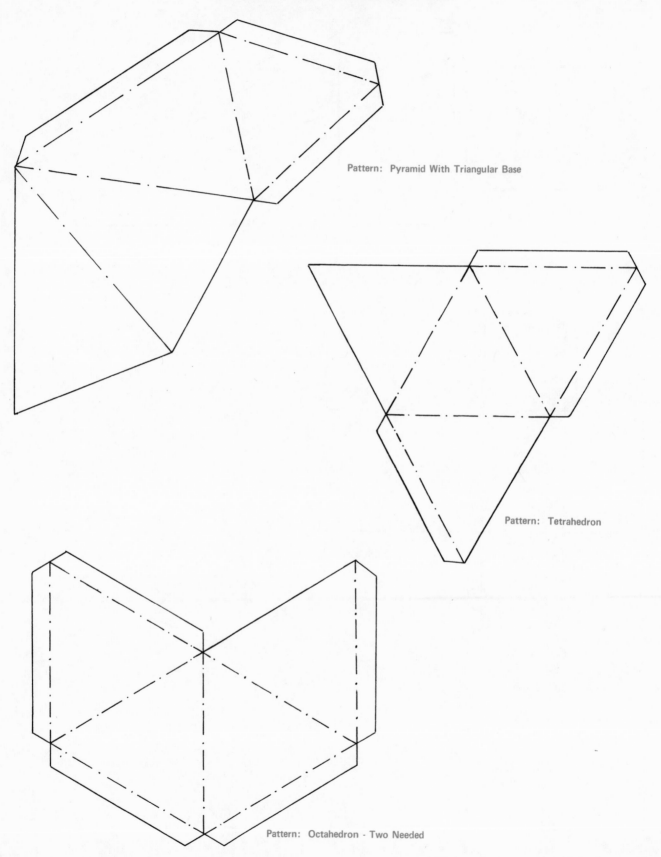

Pattern: Pyramid With Triangular Base

Pattern: Tetrahedron

Pattern: Octahedron - Two Needed

PATTERNS FOR GEOMETRIC SOLIDS

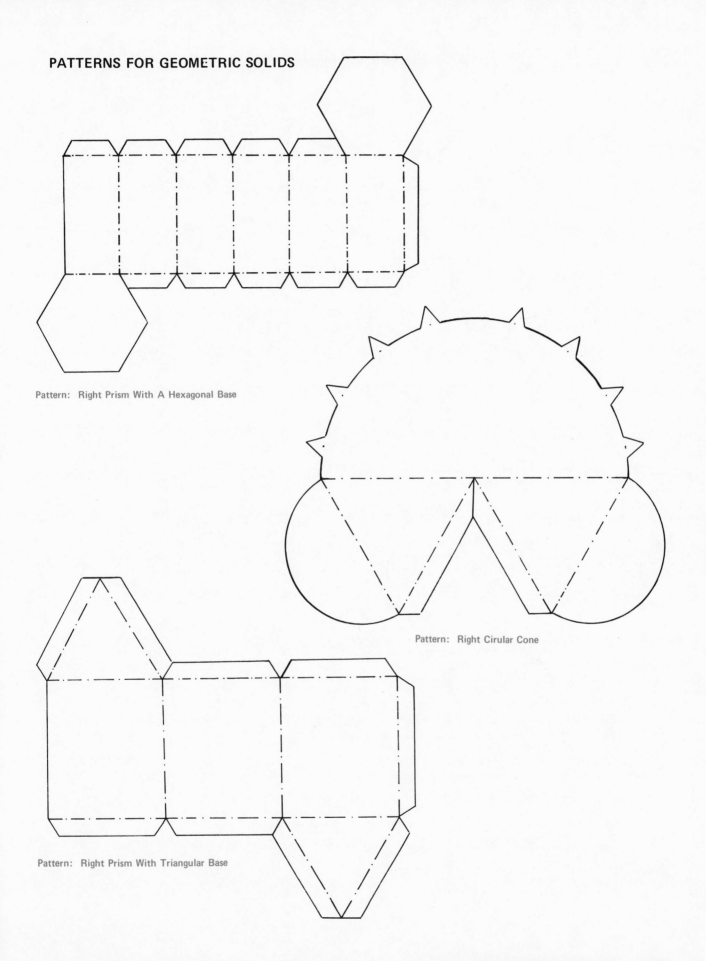

Pattern: Right Prism With A Hexagonal Base

Pattern: Right Cirular Cone

Pattern: Right Prism With Triangular Base

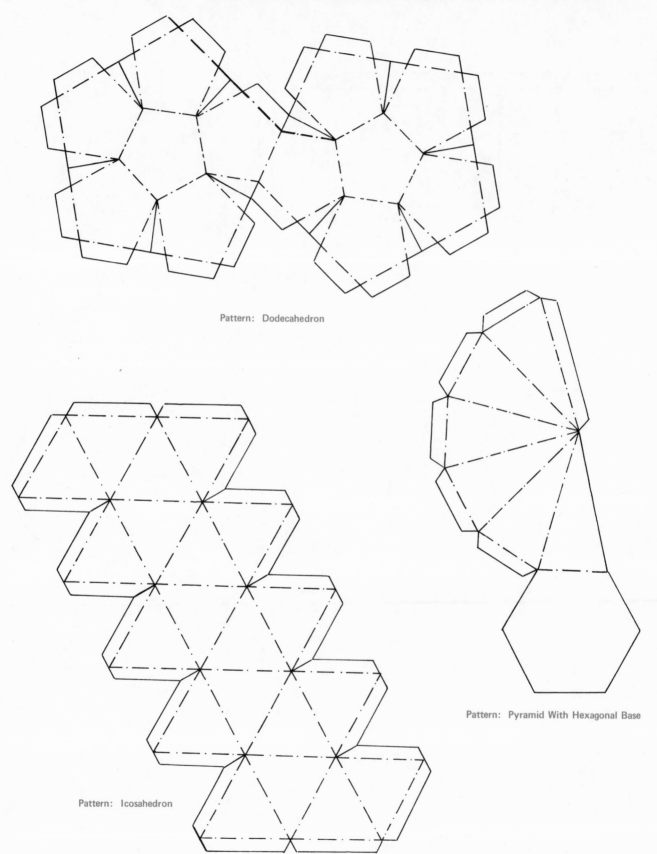

Pattern: Dodecahedron

Pattern: Pyramid With Hexagonal Base

Pattern: Icosahedron

For transparent models, cut the pages containing patterns from the manual and use the drawings to copy the shapes onto thermal film (such as Thermo-Fax 588 film). A film producing a *black line* on *color background* is especially good. For printing directions see Heat-Duplication Transparencies or Master Transparencies, pp. 13–19. Cut the patterns out, fold, and tape together with transparent tape.

A "ditto" master may be made directly from the patterns using either a Thermo-Fax machine and master or a Masterfax machine and thermal master. Ledger paper or construction paper may be cut to size and printed from the master, providing enough prints for all students to use if desired. Cut the patterns out, fold, and paste together.

For large models, project the patterns onto cardboard using an opaque projector. Then trace, cut out, fold, and glue together.

WEATHER INSTRUMENTS

Several simple weather instruments, which will help to stimulate interest in a study of weather, can easily be constructed by either students or the teacher. Five kinds of weather instrument are described and illustrated on the following pages.

ANEMOMETER

A model anemometer, or wind gauge, is easily made from readily available materials and can be used to estimate wind speed.

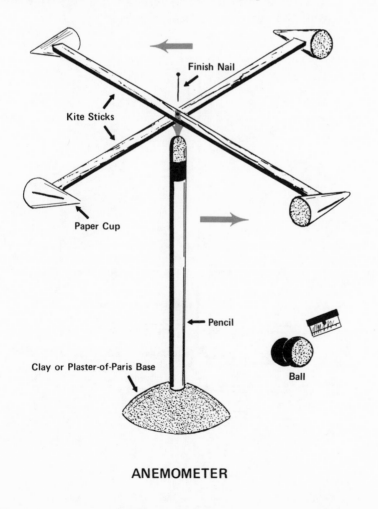

Finish Nail

Kite Sticks

Paper Cup

Pencil

Ball

Clay or Plaster-of-Paris Base

ANEMOMETER

four conical paper cups (*Note:* halves of two small hollow rubber balls or ping-pong balls may be used in place of cups if desired)
two kite sticks or other small light sticks, approximately 1′ long
one pencil with an eraser still intact
small finish nail
ball of clay or plaster of Paris to serve as a base for the anemometer
household cement
hammer
petroleum jelly or machine oil

Procedure

Glue paper cups to the ends of two sticks (or cut two balls in half) and glue each cup to the sticks as illustrated. Cross the sticks and glue together with household cement. When the cement dries, make a hole in the center of the cross with a finish nail. Lubricate the hole with petroleum jelly or machine oil. Nail the assembly to the end of the pencil, and secure the pencil in the clay or plaster of Paris. The anemometer is now ready to use.

If the anemometer turns sluggishly, enlarge the nail hole *slightly.* A very small washer or a bead on the nail between the eraser and the crossed sticks will also help, especially if it is lubricated with a drop of machine oil. A satisfactory washer can be made with a button-size piece of aluminum foil or thin smooth cardboard.

A small, light anemometer may be constructed from drinking straws and paper cups following the same general procedure outlined above.

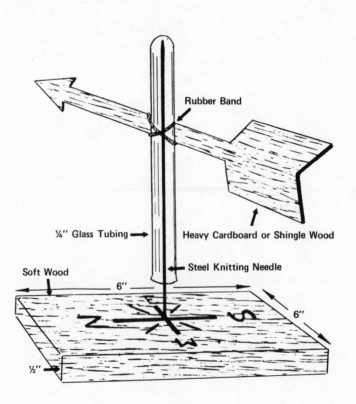

WIND VANE

WIND VANE

Construction and use of a wind vane is an interesting educational experience for students studying weather. A simple wind vane is illustrated here.

Materials and Equipment

soft wood, 6" × 6" × ¹/₂"   heavy cardboard or shingle wood
steel knitting needle   rubber band
test tube   nail or bit for making hole in wooden base

Procedure

Bore a hole in the center of the wood base. Insert a knitting needle in the hole. Make an arrow of a heavy cardboard or shingle wood and attach it to a test tube with a rubber band. Place the tube on the knitting needle and balance the vane so that it swings easily and freely. On the base, paint the letters which indicate directions.

BAROMETER

A barometer is a very useful instrument to have when a class is studying weather, regardless of the grade level of the students involved. The barometer described and illustrated in this section is very useful to both teachers and students in predicting weather from the pressure-system movements.

Note: This barometer may also respond to changes in temperature. Use *only* in the shade, *not* in direct sunlight.

Materials and Equipment

¹/₂ -gallon flat-topped milk carton or cardboard box of similar size
razor blade
sewing needle
broom straw
two paper clips
thread
thin sheet of rubber or plastic
small wide-mouthed jar
household cement or glue
penny
cardboard

Procedure

After acquiring the necessary materials and equipment, wait for a day when the barometric pressure is about average for the area in which the school is located. Then:

1. Cut an opening in the side of the box or carton large enough for the jar to pass through. Cut an H-shaped opening in the top of the carton, making the parallel cuts shorter than the length of the needle. Prepare a cardboard gauge as illustrated.

2. Tack or glue the cardboard gauge to the back of the carton. Insert the needle in the cardboard tabs as shown, and place the end of a broom straw in the eye of the needle.

3. Place the thin rubber sheet over the mouth of the jar and fasten it on tightly with a rubber band. Attach the thread to one end of a paper clip, and glue the paper clip to the center of the rubber covering.

4. Place the jar inside the carton, pull the thread up through the opening previously cut in the top of the carton, and wrap the thread twice around

BAROMETER

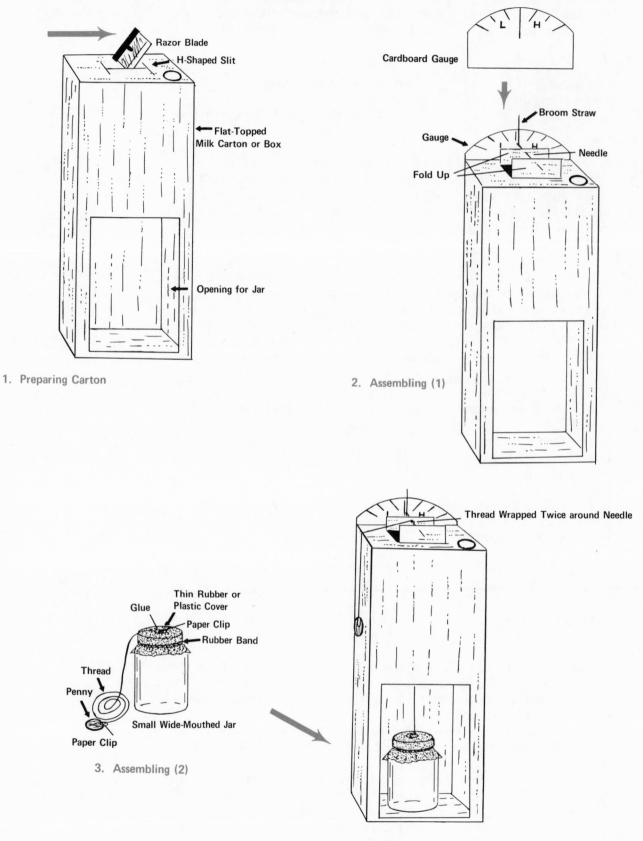

1. Preparing Carton

Razor Blade
H-Shaped Slit
Flat-Topped Milk Carton or Box
Opening for Jar

2. Assembling (1)

Cardboard Gauge
Broom Straw
Gauge
Needle
Fold Up

3. Assembling (2)

Glue
Thin Rubber or Plastic Cover
Paper Clip
Rubber Band
Thread
Penny
Paper Clip
Small Wide-Mouthed Jar

4. Finishing

Thread Wrapped Twice around Needle

the needle. Lay the free end of the thread over the side of the carton and tie it to a paper clip. Place a penny in the clip. Rotate the needle so that the straw points up.

Variations in barometric pressure will be registered by movements of the straw to the right for high pressure, and to the left for low pressure. If they are opposite in direction, rewind the thread around the needle in the opposite direction. If the needle does not turn easily, put a *small* drop of machine oil where it passes through each cardboard tab.

MECHANICAL THERMOMETER

A mechanical thermometer of the type described here is useful for indicating low and high temperatures in weather study, and in social studies for indicating temperature range in various geographical locations at different times of the year. It must be manipulated; it does not respond to changes in atmospheric temperature.

MECHANICAL THERMOMETER

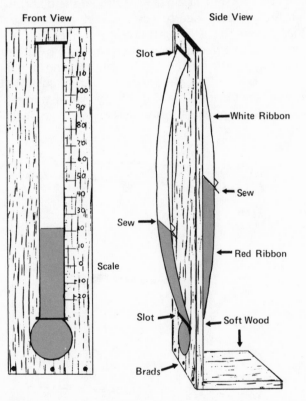

Front View Side View

Slot

White Ribbon

Sew

Sew

Red Ribbon

Scale

Slot Soft Wood

Brads

Materials and Equipment

> piece of red ribbon or elastic, and a piece of white ribbon or elastic
> heavy cardboard or soft wood
> pen to be used in drawing a temperature scale
> needle and thread
> brads or small nails, if a base is to be used
> knife or razor blade for cutting slots in the thermometer face

Procedure

Cut the front of the thermometer to size. Draw on it the outline of the bulb and the temperature scale. Paint the bulb red to match the ribbon, or paste in some ribbon to fill the outline. Cut one slot above the scale and another slot below the scale, wide enough to accommodate the ribbons. Attach the ribbons as illustrated. Nail the thermometer to a base if desired.

HYGROMETERS

Relative humidity is an important determiner of precipitation possibilities, and should be studied and measured by students engaged in weather study. Two simple, effective, easily constructed hygrometers are described and illustrated here.

Materials and Equipment for a Wet-Bulb Hygrometer

one ½ -gallon milk carton	razor blade
two thermometers	small jar
rubber band	old tubular shoe lace with ends removed

Procedure

Cut an opening in the side of the carton large enough for the jar. Attach two thermometers to the carton with a rubber band as illustrated. Cut a slot large enough for the shoe lace to pass through immediately below the thermometer located on the side of the carton. Place a small jar full of water inside the carton. Take a shoe lace, open one end of it, and slip it over the bulb of the thermometer on the side of the carton, or wrap the end of the shoe lace around the bulb of the thermometer as illustrated. Place the other end of the shoe lace through the slot into the jar of water. The shoe lace will act as a wick and keep one thermometer bulb wet. When the humidity is

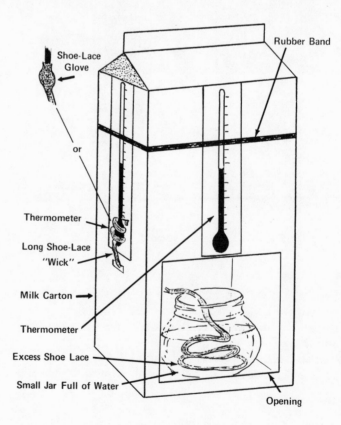

WET-BULB HYGROMETER

very high, there will be little or no difference in the readings of the thermometers. During dry weather, the water will evaporate, cooling the bulb, thus lowering the temperature registered on the wet-bulb thermometer. The temperature registered on the second thermometer will not be affected by humidity change, thus causing a difference in what the two thermometers register during dry weather. The lower the humidity, the greater the difference.

Materials and Equipment for a Hair Hygrometer

quart milk carton, flat-top type, or box of similar size
razor blade
sewing needle
broom straw
two paper clips
clean, long human hair
two pennies
cardboard

1. Preparing Components

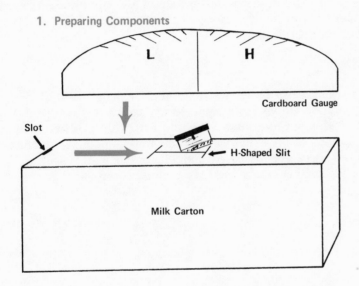

2. Assembling and Finishing

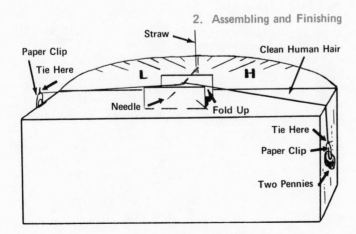

HAIR HYGROMETER

After acquiring the necessary materials and equipment, wait for a day when the relative humidity is average for the area in which the school is located. Then:

1. Cut an H-shaped opening in the side near the center of the carton, making the parallel cuts shorter than the length of the needle. Prepare a cardboard gauge as illustrated.

2. Tack or glue the cardboard gauge to the back of the carton. Insert the needle in the cardboard tabs as shown, and place the end of a broom straw in the eye of the needle. Cut a slot at one end of the carton, and insert a paper clip as illustrated. Tie or glue a long clean human hair to the paper clip, wrap the hair twice around the needle, and attach the other end of the hair to another paper clip. Place two pennies in the paper clip and suspend over the end of the carton.

During damp weather, the hair will become saturated with moisture and expand, causing the needle to move to the right, indicating higher relative humidity. During dry weather, the hair will contract and cause the needle to move to the left, indicating lower relative humidity. If the needle moves in the contrary directions, rewind the hair in the opposite direction. If the needle moves with difficulty, put a *small* drop of machine oil where it goes through the cardboard tabs.

COMPASSES

Students may get a better understanding of magnetism and how a compass works if they are given an opportunity to make a compass themselves. With little equipment and know-how, students can produce compasses that are quite acceptable for teaching fundamentals of compass operation. Three types of compasses are discussed and illustrated in this section: a floating compass, a balanced compass, and a suspended compass.

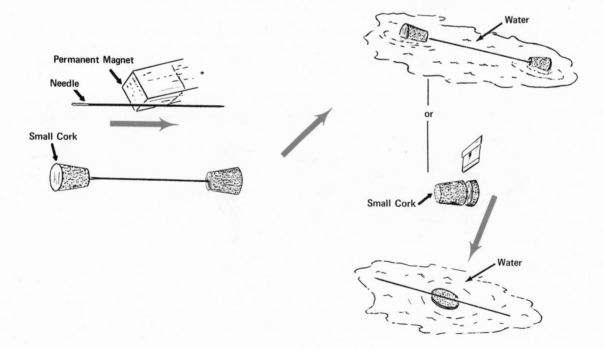

FLOATING COMPASS

FLOATING COMPASS

Materials and Equipment

permanent magnet
large sewing needle
two corks

sharp razor blade
cup or bowl of water
indelible-ink pen

Procedure

Lay the materials out in an orderly fashion on a table or desk top. Then:

1. Pick up the sewing needle and stroke it in *one* direction *only* with one pole (or end) of a permanent magnet.

2. Stick two small corks on the needle, one on each end, or slice off a thin piece of cork.

3. Place the needle with corks on both ends in the cup or bowl of water, or place the magnetized needle on the slice of cork, and float in the cup or bowl of water. The magnetized needle will soon point along the magnetic north-south line. Mark the corks N and S to show which direction is north and which south.

BALANCED COMPASS

Materials and Equipment

medicine dropper
long finish nail and hammer
board to serve as a base
cork or stopper with a hole in it
two darning or knitting needles
permanent magnet
pen and ink, or paints

Procedure

Saw the base to size, and hammer a nail down through the center of the base. Insert the medicine dropper in the hole in the cork or rubber stopper. Magnetize the two needles, stroking in *one* direction *only*. Stroke from the eye to the point of one needle and from the point to the eye of the other needle. Insert the needle in the cork as illustrated. Balance this assembly on the nail; in a few seconds the needle will align on the magnetic north-south

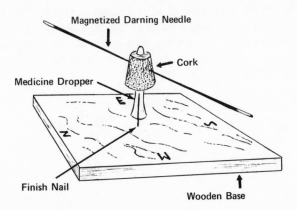

Magnetized Darning Needle

Cork

Medicine Dropper

Finish Nail

Wooden Base

BALANCED COMPASS

SUSPENDED COMPASS

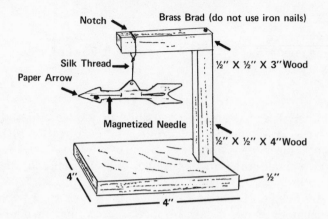

Notch

Brass Brad (do not use iron nails)

Silk Thread

Paper Arrow

½" X ½" X 3" Wood

Magnetized Needle

½" X ½" X 4" Wood

4"

½"

4"

line. Mark the appropriate needle eye to indicate north (a colored thread will do it, or a drop of nail polish; or mark the cork top). On the base, draw or paint N, S, E, and W as in the illustration.

SUSPENDED COMPASS

Materials and Equipment

one ½ " X ½ " X 3" piece of wood
one ½ " X ½ " X 4" piece of wood
one 4" X 4" X ½ " piece of wood
several brass brads (iron nails will not do) and a hammer
piece of paper, and scissors
sewing needle
thread
permanent magnet
knife or razor blade

Procedure

Saw the base and suspension pieces to size and assemble with brass brads. Cut a notch in the wooden suspension arm. Magnetize the needle by stroking it in *one* direction *only* with a permanent magnet. Cut an arrow from a piece of paper, and insert the magnetized needle through two slots cut in the arrow. Hang the arrow with thread as illustrated. The needle may be moved toward or away from the point of the arrow so that the arrow will balance properly while suspended. The arrow will point to magnetic north or south in a few seconds; if it points south, turn the needle ends in the opposite direction.

Display and Study of Live Specimens

VI

The study of live specimens can do much to promote interest in life science. Students may become directly involved in the care and feeding of insects, fish, and animals on display, and they can develop, with teacher guidance, an orderly approach to the observation of live specimens.

An attempt has been made to include in this chapter representative devices for the display and study of live specimens. Presented here are insect cages, including an insect-study case; a vivarium (or ant home); an animal cage; a four-sided terrarium; two jar terrariums; a jar aquarium; an aquarium, funnel, and fish trap; an electric bottle cutter useful in making jar aquariums; and a seed-germination case.

INSECT CAGES

Although insects captured, killed, and preserved are often very useful in science education, at times live specimens will be even more useful to an enterprising teacher. Four insect cages are illustrated here. All allow students to see insects in action.

SHOE-BOX INSECT CAGE

A shoe-box cage for insects may be made by teachers or students following these suggestions and accompanying illustrations.

Materials and Equipment

shoe box
glass pane or clear acetate (plastic)
masking tape
knife or razor blade
scissors
glass cutter (if glass is used)

milk carton, $\frac{1}{2}$ pt.
water
plant
pins
screening

SHOE-BOX CAGE

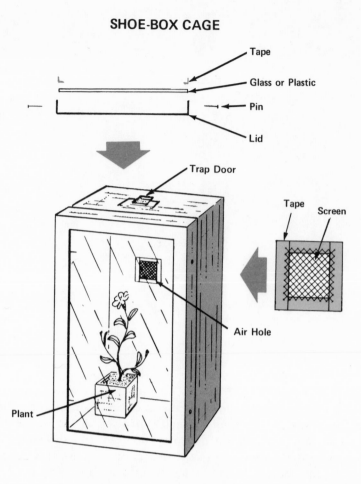

Procedure

1. Lay out the window area of the box lid; window glass or plastic should have ½″ margin of lid on all sides.

2. Cut the window area.

3. Tape the glass pane or plastic to the inside of the box lid; use enough tape to provide rigidity.

4. Cut a trap door in the top end of the cage as illustrated to allow for easy placement of insects into the finished cage; secure this door with tape.

5. Cut a small hole in the bottom (back) of the box and tape a piece of wire screen over this air hole.

6. Put a plant in the milk carton and place it in the box.

7. Put live insects in the cage.

8. Pin the lid to the box (see illustration).

OATMEAL-BOX INSECT CAGE

A round cereal box or ice-cream carton can be easily and quickly made into a cage for use in the study of various insects. This cage has a ready-made door—the box lid—through which it is easy to place insects, food, and other essentials into the cage.

Materials and Equipment

round cereal box or ice-cream carton   tin snips or old scissors
screening   razor blade or sharp knife
cloth tape

OATMEAL-BOX INSECT CAGE

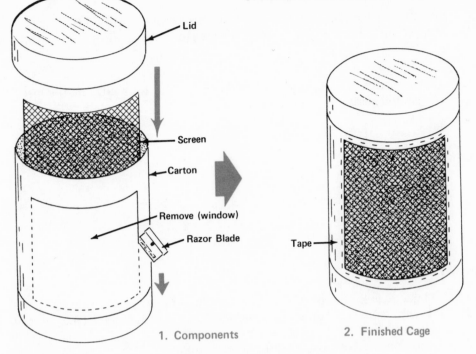

Lid

Screen

Carton

Remove (window)

Razor Blade

Tape

1. Components

2. Finished Cage

Procedure

1. Cut the window in the side of the box, leaving the box lid in place to afford more rigidity and make the cutting easier.

2. Cut the wire screen somewhat larger than the window it is to cover.

3. Tape the screen to the box.

The cage is now ready to receive insect inhabitants.

JAR CAGE

A jar cage is probably the simplest cage to construct if the materials are available.

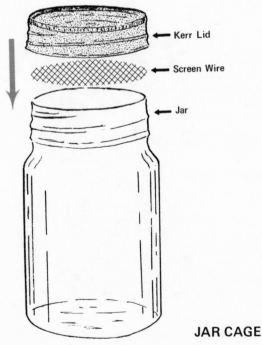

Kerr Lid

Screen Wire

Jar

JAR CAGE

Materials and Equipment

    wide-mouth glass jar   galvanized wire cut to lid size
    Kerr jar lid to fit   shears (for cutting wire)

Procedure

Cut the screen wire to size and insert inside the Kerr lid. Put the insect into the jar and screw the lid on tight.

JAR-LID SCREEN-WIRE CAGE

Materials and Equipment

    two mayonnaise-jar lids
    one piece of wire screening 12″ × 12″
    stapler (regular desk type)
    tin snips
    masking tape

Procedure

1. Make a cylinder of the screening, allowing for a 1″ overlap to be fastened with staples. Adjust the cylinder so that the open ends of the cylinder will fit into the jar lids.
2. Tape the exposed edges of the screen cylinder.
3. Staple the overlap securely.
4. Fit the mayonnaise-jar lids on each end of the screen cylinder.
5. Stand the cylinder upright.

Explanation

This same procedure can be applied in making cages for animals larger than insects if heavier materials are used. Cake tins may replace mayonnaise-

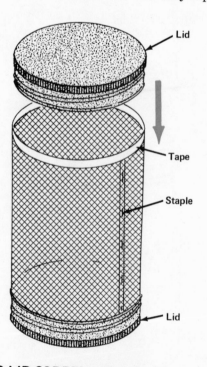

JAR-LID SCREEN-WIRE CAGE

jar lids and hardware cloth of about ¼" mesh may be used instead of screening. It may also be prudent to place a brick on top of the cage to increase the stability of the upright cylinder.

INSECT-STUDY CASE

A glass study case is useful for studying various burrowing insects, and is also useful for observing a colony of termites at work.

Materials and Equipment

two pieces of window glass
three wooden strips, slightly wider than the specimen to be placed in the
  case (if burrowing insects are to be displayed)
roll of wide plastic, adhesive, or masking tape

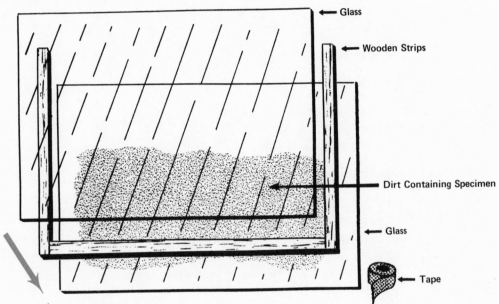

1. Components

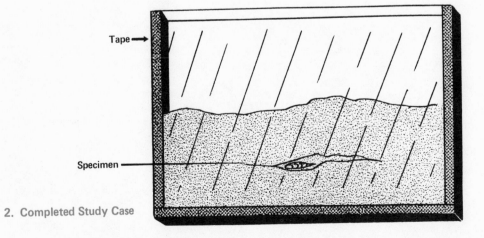

2. Completed Study Case

INSECT-STUDY CASE

Lay a piece of glass flat on a table. Place dirt containing the live specimen or a damp, rotted piece of wood containing the termites, on the glass. Lay wooden strips cut to size (slightly wider than the specimen to be displayed) around the edges of one piece of glass, as illustrated. Place a second piece of glass on the top of the wooden strips and tape together. A display case for burrowing insects generally requires no cover. A termite display should be covered by taping a wooden strip over the opening so that the insects will not escape. Keep the case enclosed in dark cloth or paper except when observing the insects.

TERRARIUMS

JAR TERRARIUM

A jar terrarium will serve nicely for displaying small specimens, and is easier to construct than a larger four-sided terrarium. Two types are illustrated.

Materials and Equipment (Type 1)

> screen wire
> small piece of wood, 1″ × 6″ × 6″
> two screws, 1¼″ or 1½″ in length
> screw-driver
> small nail
> hammer
> tin snips or shears (to cut the screen wire)
> jar

Procedure

1. Hammer the nail through the lid to make a number of air holes.
2. Cut the screen wire to fit *inside* the lid.
3. Use the nail to make two holes in the piece of wood.

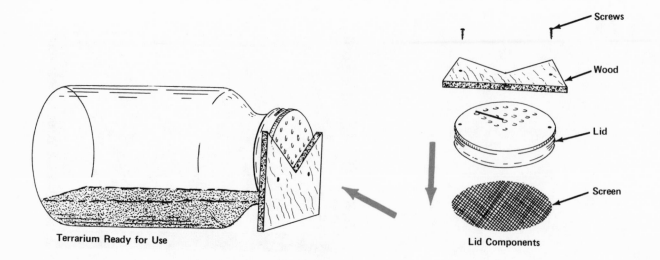

Terrarium Ready for Use

Lid Components

JAR TERRARIUM-TYPE 1

JAR-TERRARIUM-TYPE 2

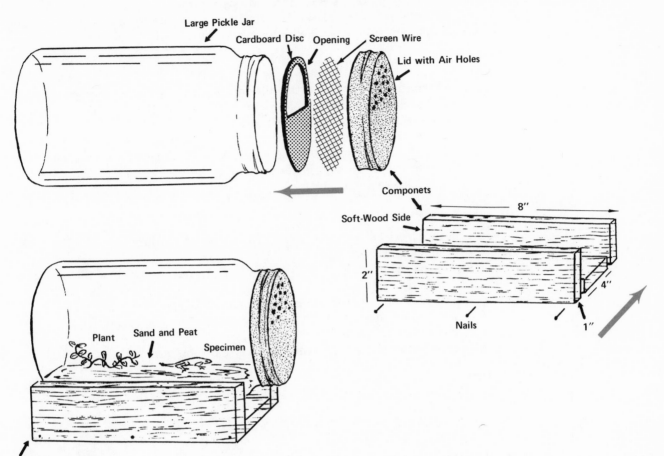

Large Pickle Jar
Cardboard Disc Opening Screen Wire
Lid with Air Holes
Componets
Soft-Wood Side
8"
2"
4"
1"
Nails

Plant Sand and Peat Specimen

Finished Terrarium

4. Cut the wood and fasten it to the lid as illustrated. Screw the lid on the jar. Place the terrarium on its side.

The terrarium is now ready for the insertion of soil and specimens. Care and stocking are the same as for the four-sided terrarium, allowing for size differences; see page 136.

Materials and Equipment (Type 2)

> large jar with lid (a pickle jar or a mayonnaise jar, one-gallon size, will do)
> galvanized screen wire cut to interior size of lid
> piece of heavy cardboard cut to interior size of lid
> one piece of wood, 1" × 4" × 8"
> two pieces of wood, each 1" × 2" × 8"
> nails
> household cement

Procedure

Nail the wooden base and sides together as shown. Prepare the lid by punching holes in it from the top side. Cut a hole in the cardboard disc as illustrated and cement the screen wire to the cardboard. Place the bottle *mouth up* on a table, put the cardboard disc on the mouth of the jar, and then put the screen disc on top of the cardboard. Then, screw the lid into place. Lay the jar on its side in the wooden frame.

Stocking and care of the jar terrarium is essentially the same as for the four-sided terrarium described later except on a smaller scale.

FOUR-SIDED TERRARIUM

A terrarium is a very worthwhile addition to any elementary-school classroom or secondary-school biology room because it affords students an excellent opportunity to get to know more about living plants and animals. Student interest in nature study may be greatly stimulated by using student committees or making individual assignments in regard to stocking and care of the terrarium. A simple terrarium can be easily constructed by either older students or the teacher.

Materials and Equipment

> four pieces of glass, 9″ × 12″ for a large terrarium, or 6″ × 10″ for a small terrarium
>
> two pieces of glass, 9″ × 9″ for a large terrarium, or 6″ × 6″ for a small terrarium
>
> two rolls of 2″ plastic, masking, or adhesive tape
>
> eight safety matches with heads removed
>
> hasp
>
> glass cutter (if glass must be cut to size by the teacher)

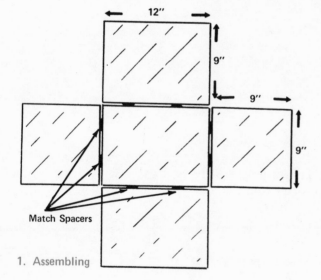

1. Assembling

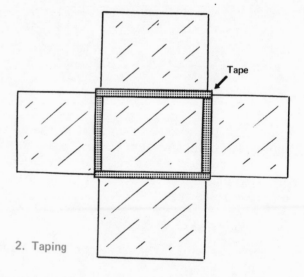

2. Taping

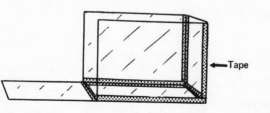

3. Folding

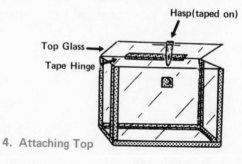

4. Attaching Top

FOUR-SIDED TERRARIUM

Procedure

Secure materials needed for construction. Glass scraps may be available free of charge from some glass companies. Have glass cut to the desired size or cut the glass to the proper size.

Suggestions for cutting glass: (a) mark dimensions of the glass pieces on a sheet of paper; (b) place glass over the paper sheet; (c) position a ruler (tape it to the glass if necessary—it must not slip) on top of the glass along the line marked on the sheet of paper and score along this line with a glass cutter, holding the glass cutter against the ruler as the glass is cut; (d) place the glass over the edge of a table with the scored line *face up*. Downward pressure on the glass should cause it to break at the scored line. Then:

1. After all pieces of glass have been cut to size, lay the assembly on a table as illustrated, with one of the four larger pieces of glass placed to one side for later use as a lid. Insert matches between the glass sheets as illustrated.

2. Tape the ends and sides to the base with plastic, masking, or adhesive tape.

3. Carefully turn the entire assembly over, and remove the matches from between the glass sheets. Fold *one end* up and place the edge *flat on the table*, against the bottom or base sheet of glass. Pull up *one side* and place *on top* of the edge of the glass base. Tape the side and end piece together. Pull the other end up, and place the edge of the other end firmly on the table, and tape into place. Tape the remaining side piece into place to complete the open glass box.

4. Attach the top or cover glass to the open glass box with a strip of adhesive tape approximately ten inches long. Cover all of the glass edges of the terrarium with tape so that hands will not be cut while working with animals. Attach a hasp with tape to hold the lid in place if desired.

Stocking and Care of the Terrarium

Cover the bottom with clean gravel, sand, and peat. Choose attractive rocks and small potted plants, or plants such as shield fern, creeping snowberry, or polytrichum moss, and place in the bottom of the terrarium. The terrarium is now ready to receive animal guests. Clean the terrarium at least once a week. (*Note*: Variations in the stocking of the terrarium should be made when needed so that the animal's terrarium environment will conform as closely as possible to the environment found in nature.)

AQUARIUMS

GALLON-JAR AQUARIUM

A gallon-jar aquarium may be prepared for use in observing simple animal life with a minimum of materials and expense.

Materials and Equipment

gallon jar
pane of glass or saucer for cover
pebbles (gravel)

elodea (plant)
animal specimen

Procedure

Place pebbles in the jar, and anchor the plants in place. A generous amount of plant life and a minimal number of animals will provide a bal-

GALLON-JAR AQUARIUM

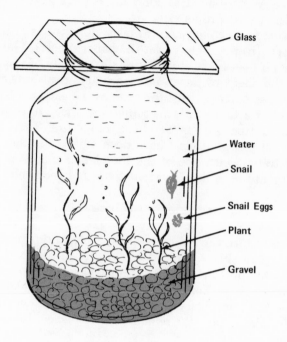

anced aquarium (about 15 cubic inches of water to 1 inch of animal length is a good ratio).

Rather than making one aquarium too crowded, several aquaria can be set up, each housing a different animal form. These will provide more numerous observational activities for children.

Having a snail in an aquarium affords close up views of the animal and the eggs it may lay on the inside of the jar. Snail eggs are translucent and the anatomy of the developing young can be studied under a hand lens (magnifying glass).

AQUARIUM, FUNNEL, AND FISH TRAP

All three of these devices may be constructed from a glass jug, and will find many uses in the elementary-school classroom or biological-science laboratory. Students should be taught to care for the aquarium and to procure animals for classroom study.

Materials and Equipment

    glass cutter
    gallon jug
    desk drawer or box slightly wider than the diameter of the jug
    sharp knife
    device for the breaking of the top of the jug from the bottom after
        scoring with the glass cutter: a coat hanger and nut; or string, lighter
        fluid, and water; or an electric bottle cutter (construction and use of
        an electric bottle cutter will be found following the discussion of
        aquarium construction)
    sandpaper or file
    materials for stocking the aquarium

AQUARIUM, FUNNEL, AND FISH TRAP

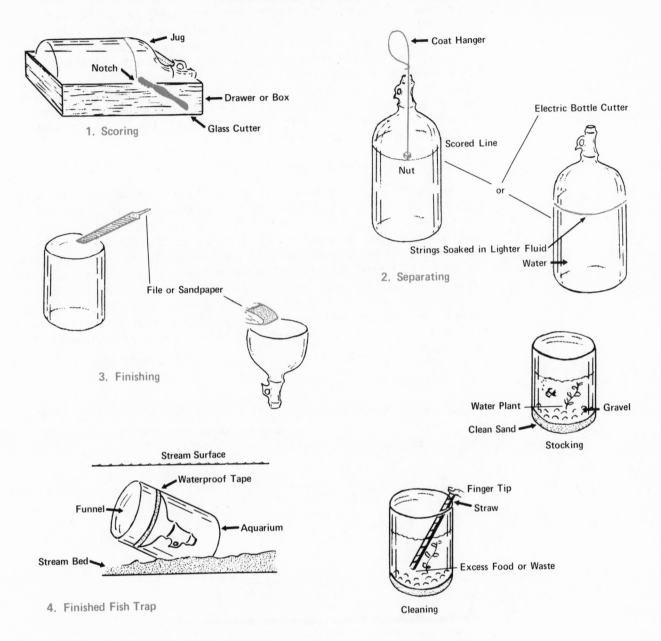

1. Scoring

Jug
Notch
Drawer or Box
Glass Cutter

2. Separating

Coat Hanger
Electric Bottle Cutter
Scored Line
Nut
Strings Soaked in Lighter Fluid
Water

3. Finishing

File or Sandpaper

Stocking

Water Plant
Gravel
Clean Sand

4. Finished Fish Trap

Stream Surface
Waterproof Tape
Funnel
Aquarium
Stream Bed

Cleaning

Finger Tip
Straw
Excess Food or Waste

Procedure

Secure all needed materials. Then:

1. Place the gallon jug in the desk drawer (or box) with the bottom of the jug held firmly against the end of the drawer. It is advisable to get a student or friend to help hold the jug in place. Draw a line with a pencil on the side of the drawer approximately 2″ below the base of the neck of the jug. Cut a notch in the drawer, place the glass cutter in the notch, and have the assistant rotate the jar downward against the glass cutter.

2. Now separate the jug top (funnel) from the body of the jug (the aquarium). Take a coat hanger and attach the nut to the end of it as shown. Tap against the scored line inside the bottle until the glass begins to chip. Continue tapping all the way around until the bottle top breaks free. An-

other way to remove the jug top is to fill the jug to the scored line with water, wrap a string around the scored line, soak the string with lighter fluid or turpentine, and set on fire. The top should break loose. Still another method of breaking the top off the bottle is to use an electric bottle cutter.

3. Smooth off any rough or sharp edges on both the aquarium and funnel with a file or sandpaper.

4. To make a fish trap, place the funnel inside the aquarium and tape the two components together. Face the trap toward the source of the stream in shallow water. Small water animals will swim into the funnel and thence through it into the aquarium portion of the trap.

Stocking and Care of the Aquarium

Place a thin layer of clean sand in the bottom of the aquarium. Cover the layer of sand with a thin layer of gravel or rocks. Place water plants and a fish or two in the aquarium. (*Note*: When placing fish into the aquarium, take care to see that the temperature of the water in the aquarium is approximately the same as the temperature of the water in the container in which the fish came.) Feed the fish once a day and remove any excess food not eaten by the fish in a short period of time. To remove food or waste from the aquarium, place one end of a drinking straw on excess food or waste, cover the other end of the straw with a finger tip, and remove the straw from the water. Excess food or waste will be picked up in the water removed from the aquarium by the straw.

ELECTRIC BOTTLE CUTTER

An electric bottle cutter can make bottle-aquarium construction much less difficult. Construction of an electric bottle cutter can be accomplished with little expense by the teacher.

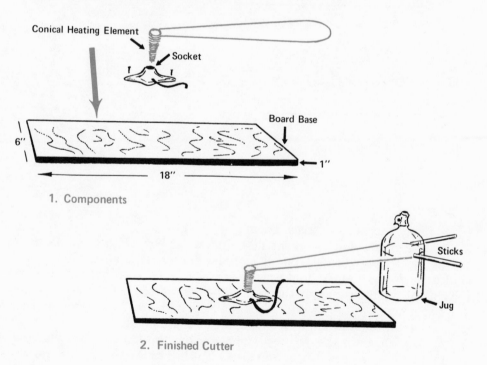

1. Components

2. Finished Cutter

ELECTRIC BOTTLE CUTTER

conical heating element (600- or 1000-watt)
screw base socket and cord
18″ board, 1″ × 6″
screws to fasten socket to board
screw driver and hammer
pliers
sticks

1. Uncoil a few turns of wire from the top of the conical heating element and shape the wire into an oval shape with pliers. Fasten the socket to the board with screws and screw the heating element into the socket.

2. With a glass cutter, score a line around the bottle as directed in the procedure for making an aquarium, funnel, and fish trap.

3. Turn the heating element on and hold with the heating element wire on the scored line. Use sticks to keep the wire in place. As the bottle cracks, rotate it slowly until the top has broken free. (*Note*: It is advisable to use an assistant to help hold the bottle-cutter board base so that it will not slip or slide. This bottle cutter should be used only by the teacher with care. It is *unsafe* for children.)

SEED-GERMINATION CASE

A seed-germination case will prove to be a very interesting and motivating device for children undertaking a study of necessary conditions for germination of seeds, difference in germination times, growth rates and stages, and other botanical phenomena.

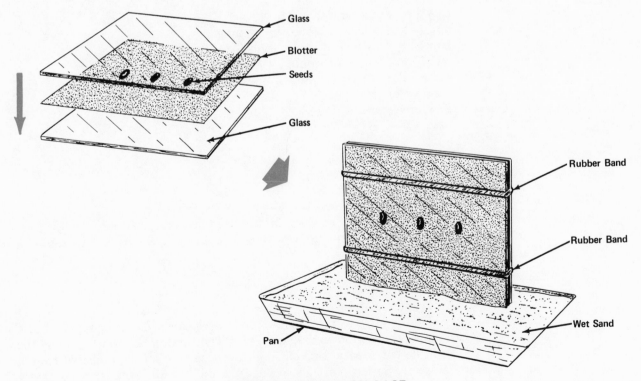

SEED-GERMINATION CASE

shallow pan (a baking pan works well)
sand
rubber bands
blotter
seeds
water
glass panes

Procedure

1. Cut the glass, or use small, precut panes. *Be sure to smooth the edges*, or *tape around them*, to avoid cutting hands of curious children.

2. Wet the blotter, and place it on *top* of a pane of glass. Lay several seeds on the blotter.

3. Place the second pane of glass on top of the blotter and seeds. Use rubber bands to hold the assembly together.

4. Partly fill the baking pan with wet sand.

5. Place the panes in the sand as shown in the illustration. Wait for the seeds to sprout, having teams of children observe and record stages of development.

VIVARIUM

A vivarium or ant home is easy to build and will help teachers provide many enjoyable and useful experiences for interested students. Since ants are easy to keep and study, both teachers and students will find the vivarium to their liking.

Materials and Equipment

two pieces of glass, 10″ × 16″
one 1″ × 4″ piece of wood, 15½″ long
two 1″ × 4″ pieces of wood, each 11½″ long
one 1″ × 4″ piece of wood, 17½″ long
assortment of wood screws or nails
hammer or screw driver
fine screen wire 3″ × 11″
hasp
hinge
household cement
stapler and staples
keyhole saw
glass cutter (if glass must be cut to size by the teacher)
device for cutting grooves in the wooden frame (wood carving tool, power saw, or rabbeting plane—a knife will do if no other tool is available)

Procedure

Arrange the materials on a flat working surface. Then:

1. Cut the glass to the desired size if necessary. (See paragraph 1 under Procedure of the section on the Four-Sided Terrarium, page 136.) Usually the glass will be cut to size for you free of charge when it is purchased from a lumber yard. Smooth off sharp edges carefully with sandpaper or emery cloth. Prepare the wooden ends and bottom by cutting two 1″ × 4″ pieces of

VIVARIUM

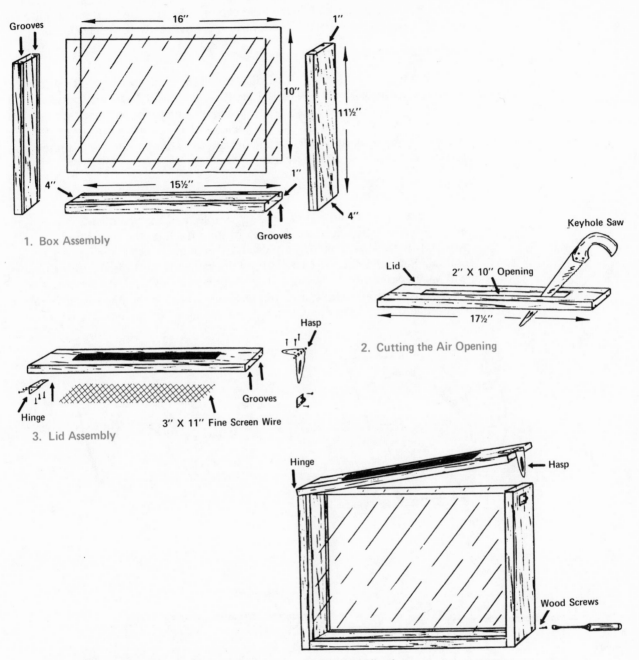

1. Box Assembly

2. Cutting the Air Opening

3. Lid Assembly

4. Finished Vivarium

wood to a length of 11½″, and one piece to a length of 15½″. Cut two lengthwise parallel grooves in each piece of wood, ¼″ deep and approximately ⅛″ wide, about 3″ apart.

2. Cut a 1″ × 4″ lid 17½″ long. Cut grooves in the lid in the same manner as the frame. A 2″ × 10″ opening should be cut in the lid with a keyhole saw or similar cutting tool.

3. Attach screen wire to the bottom of the lid, covering the opening in the board. Use a stapler to fasten the wire in place, and trim away any excess wire covering the grooves in the lid. Attach a hasp and a hinge as illustrated.

4. Assemble the frame with wood screws or nails, being careful to keep the grooves facing inward. Insert the glass sides from the top, and seal them to the wooden frame with household cement. Attach the hinges to the frame and align the hasp properly. The vivarium is now ready to receive ants.

Stocking the Vivarium and Caring for the Ants

Fill the vivarium ³/₄ full of dirt dug from an active ant hill. Shake the vivarium gently to level the dirt. Keep the dirt moist (but not too wet), and occasionally feed the ants by dropping in some moist sugar and bread crumbs. Keep the sides of the box enclosed in a dark cloth except when observing the ants at work, to encourage the ants to dig their tunnels and rooms near the sides of the vivarium.

ANIMAL CAGE

Construction of an animal cage is simple, and many educational experiences based on the care and feeding of an animal in the classroom are well worth the time and effort involved in making a cage and caring for an animal. Several types of cages can be constructed, and dimensions of cages will vary according to the size of the animals to be housed within the cage. Cage-construction details and dimensions of the cage illustrated here are suggestive only. *Note*: Do *not* use wooden cages for the housing of rodents.

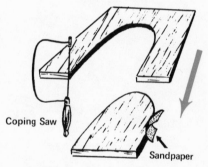

Coping Saw
Sandpaper
1. Cutting the Opening

Hinges
2. Fastening
Hook

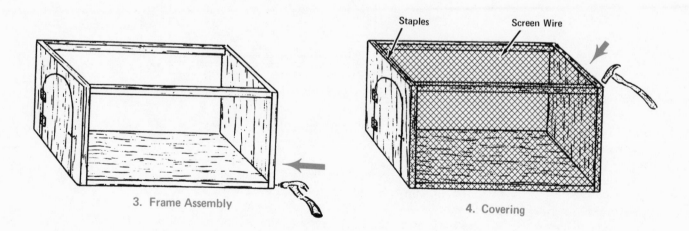

3. Frame Assembly

Staples
Screen Wire
4. Covering

ANIMAL CAGE

two pieces of plywood 12" × 12"
one piece of plywood, 12" × 24"
sandpaper
assorted nails or wood screws
2" × 2" wood, 2' long
hammer, coping saw, and screw driver
wire staples
26" × 36" screen wire or ½" mesh hardware cloth, 26" × 36"
hinges
hook and eye

Procedure

Secure all needed materials, then:

1. Cut an opening in one piece of 12" × 12" plywood with the coping saw. The piece of wood cut out will serve as a door. Remove the door and sandpaper the opening and door so that no rough edges are exposed to injure the animals or the hands of children handling the animals.

2. Attach hinges to the door; then, fasten the hinges to the door frame. With the door closed, attach the hook and eye as illustrated.

3. Nail the end pieces to the bottom, then nail the 2" × 2" frame pieces into place.

4. Use the hammer and wire staples to fasten the screen or hardware cloth to the frame. When nailing the covering to the frame, work from the *bottom* on one side to the *top* on the *same* side, across the top, and down the other side. Be sure to keep the screen or hardware cloth pulled tightly across the frame.

For information on the care and feeding of small animals, consult the nearest museum or secure information from a library.

Dramatization and Storytelling Devices

VII

There are numerous devices for dramatizing presentations and stories that can be constructed quite easily by teachers and students. Three such devices are discussed in this chapter: hand puppets and puppet stages, scroll theaters, and shadow screens.

HAND PUPPETS AND PUPPET STAGES

Dramatizations by students involving the use of puppets are very useful for promoting creative expression. A few types of basic hand puppets have been selected as representative of easily constructed, practical puppets for classroom construction and use. An illustration of a hand-puppet glove for finger or hand puppets is also included, along with two types of puppet stages. Since drawings for the puppets and puppet stages are detailed enough for teachers and students to see how each type of puppet is constructed, no written instructions are given in this section.

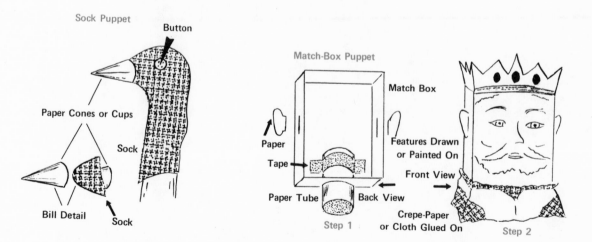

HAND PUPPETS

HAND PUPPETS

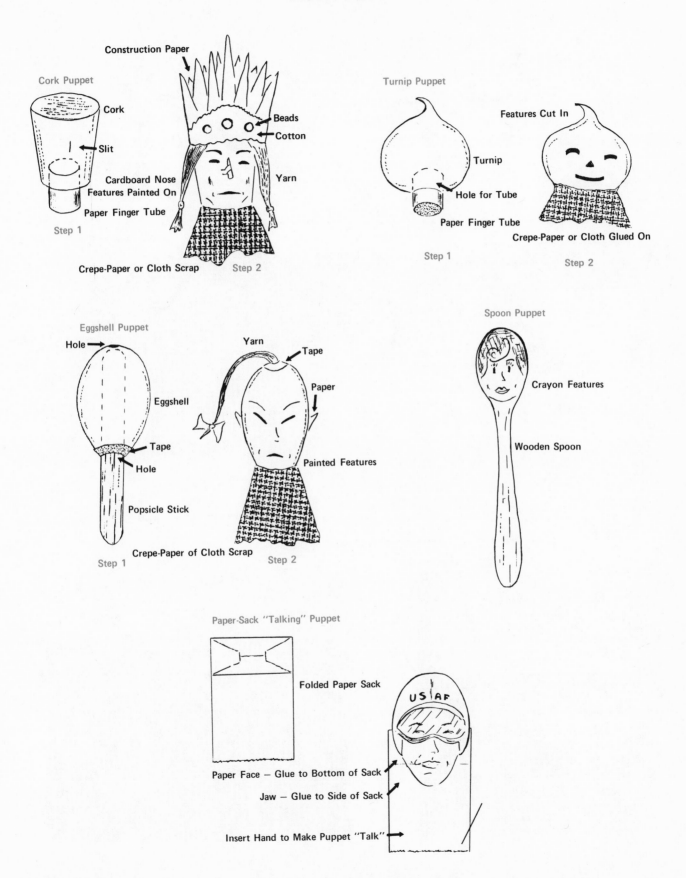

Cork Puppet

Construction Paper

Cork

Slit

Beads

Cotton

Cardboard Nose
Features Painted On

Yarn

Paper Finger Tube

Step 1

Crepe-Paper or Cloth Scrap

Step 2

Turnip Puppet

Features Cut In

Turnip

Hole for Tube

Paper Finger Tube

Step 1

Crepe-Paper or Cloth Glued On

Step 2

Eggshell Puppet

Hole

Yarn

Tape

Eggshell

Paper

Tape

Hole

Painted Features

Popsicle Stick

Crepe-Paper of Cloth Scrap

Step 1

Step 2

Spoon Puppet

Crayon Features

Wooden Spoon

Paper-Sack "Talking" Puppet

Folded Paper Sack

US AF

Paper Face — Glue to Bottom of Sack

Jaw — Glue to Side of Sack

Insert Hand to Make Puppet "Talk"

HAND PUPPETS

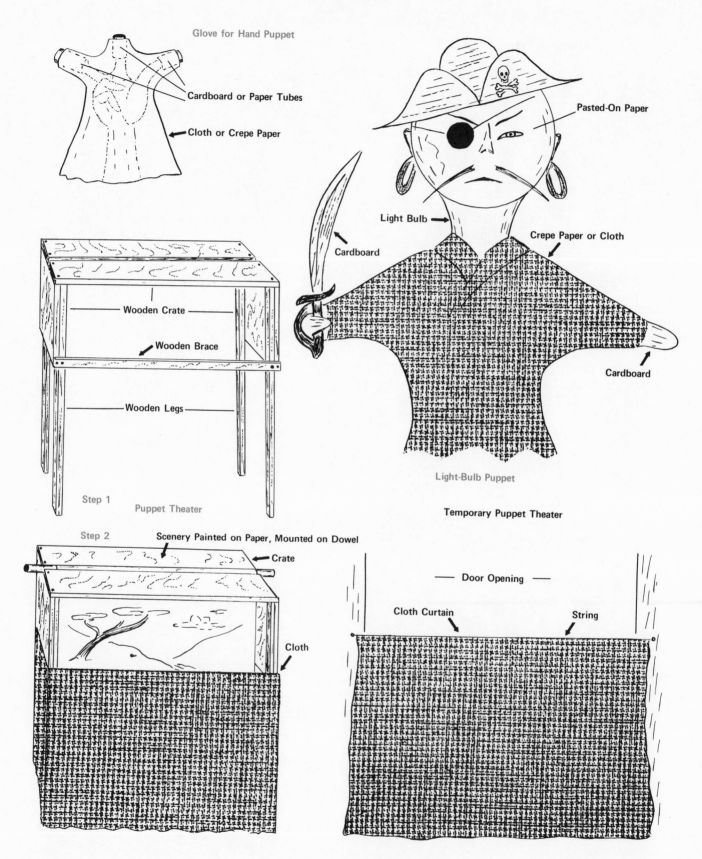

Glove for Hand Puppet

Cardboard or Paper Tubes

Cloth or Crepe Paper

Pasted-On Paper

Cardboard

Light Bulb

Crepe Paper or Cloth

Cardboard

Wooden Crate

Wooden Brace

Wooden Legs

Step 1

Puppet Theater

Light-Bulb Puppet

Temporary Puppet Theater

Step 2

Scenery Painted on Paper, Mounted on Dowel

Crate

Cloth

Door Opening

Cloth Curtain

String

HAND PUPPETS

Flip-Top Box "Talking" Puppet

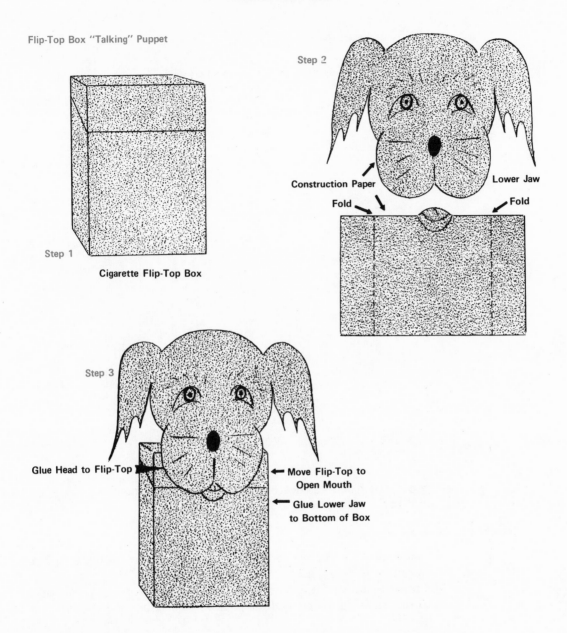

Step 1

Cigarette Flip-Top Box

Step 2

Construction Paper

Lower Jaw

Fold

Fold

Step 3

Glue Head to Flip-Top

← Move Flip-Top to
Open Mouth

← Glue Lower Jaw
to Bottom of Box

SCROLL THEATERS

The scroll theater is very useful for presenting a sequence of pictures or drawings in language-arts, social-studies, and science areas whenever a story is to be told and illustrated. Pictures are mounted or drawn on long strips of paper and rolled into view, one at a time, when needed. Pacing in presentation is controlled by the teacher or student using the device.

Two basic types of scroll theaters are presented here: the horizontal-roll theater and the vertical-roll theater.

HORIZONTAL-ROLL THEATER

Some teachers prefer the horizontal-roll theater, which is used to present pictures and drawings rolled into view horizontally. Dimensions of materials

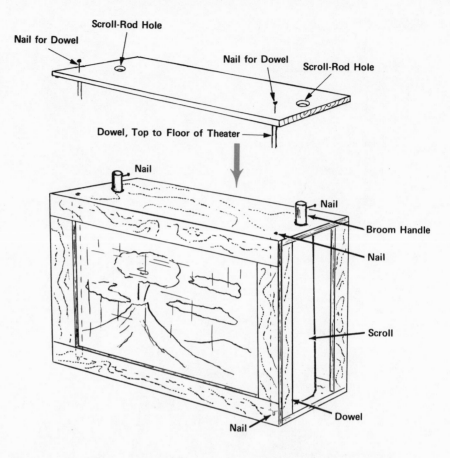

used in construction of a theater of this type are not included, since teachers may want to use dimensions to fit their specific needs.

Materials and Equipment

1″ pine, or ¹⁄₂″ plywood, for the construction of frame, top, bottom, and sides of the theater

old broom handle, for construction of scroll rods (or use ³⁄₄″ dowel)

assorted sizes of nails, including two very large ones to serve as rod handles

large finish nails

saw

hammer

strip of butcher paper for scroll

drawing and coloring instruments

small drill, or brace and bit

¹⁄₂″ diameter doweling

Procedure

Saw the top, bottom, and necessary side pieces to the desired size. Before nailing the materials together, cut holes in the top piece where the broom-handle rods are to fit. Nail the doweling into place. Be sure to cut a slot large enough to allow for insertion and removal of rod handles from the theater when changing scrolls. Hammer a large nail into the end of each broom handle as shown. Hammer a finish nail into the other end of each rod. Bore two holes, opposite the top openings, in the bottom piece of wood large enough to accommodate the finish nails in the end of each scroll rod.

Draw or paint pictures and scenes large enough to fill the theater opening, and after finishing the scroll, fasten one end to a scroll rod with pressure-sensitive tape, and roll up on the rod. Fasten the other end of the scroll to the other rod with pressure-sensitive tape, insert the rods through the opening in the back of the stage and into the appropriate holes, and present the show.

VERTICAL-ROLL THEATER

A vertical-roll theater is used to present pictures and drawings rolled into view vertically. Dimensions of materials are not given, since teachers will want to construct a theater to fulfill the individual size requirements.

Materials and Equipment

same materials listed for the horizontal-roll theater (preceding section) plus two hook-and-eye latches

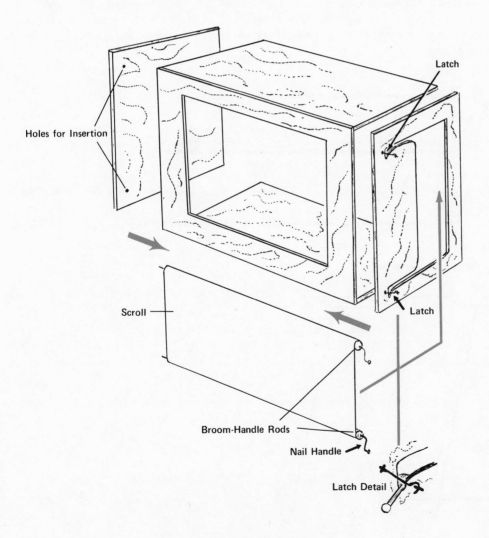

VERTICAL – ROLL THEATER

Procedure

Saw the top, bottom, and necessary side pieces to size. Before assembling the theater, saw an opening in one side piece large enough to allow for insertion of the mounted scroll. Shape the opening as illustrated. Bore two holes in the other side large enough for the finish nails in the end of the scroll rods, being sure to space properly. Bend two large nails for use as handles, and hammer into one end of each rod. Hammer a finish nail into the other end of each rod. Fasten each hook and eye on the side of the theater box as illustrated in the drawing.

The scroll is prepared and attached to the scroll rods as was suggested for the horizontal-roll theater, except the pictures must be drawn so the scroll may be rolled through vertically. Insert the mounted scroll into the theater, latch in place, and present the show.

SHADOW SCREENS

A shadow screen is most useful in language arts for developing ease and clarity of expression by allowing even the most timid of students to act out parts of a story by presenting the dramatization through cutout figures and illustrations pressed against a plastic screen. Due to the semitransparent nature of the plastic covering of the screen, the cutouts may be seen clearly by the class while the child presenting the story remains completely hidden from view.

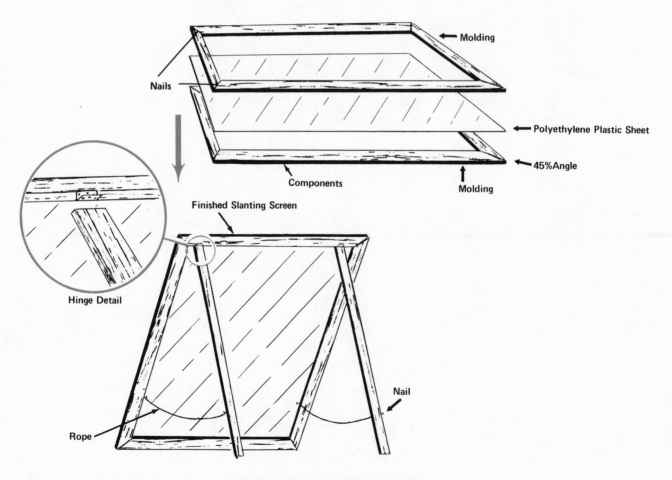

SLANTING SHADOW SCREEN

Described in detail here is the slanting shadow screen, one of the most popular of the shadow screens with teachers.

Materials and Equipment

> eight pieces of molding, 40″ long, to use in making the frame (other dimensions may be used).
>
> two pieces of 1″ × 2″ wood, 40″ long, to serve as braces
>
> two pieces of chain or rope, about 3′ long
>
> two hinges
>
> two large nails, and wood screws for mounting the hinges
>
> sheet of polyethylene plastic (frosted acetate), 42″ × 42″
>
> assorted finish nails appropriate for construction of the frame

Procedure

Cut all the material to be used in construction of the shadow screen to the desired size. Cut the eight pieces of frame board with an angle of 45° at each end to allow for joints (see illustration). Then:

1. Arrange the four pieces of frame material in the form of a square. Place the plastic sheet on the top of the first frame and nail the other frame pieces on top of the plastic. Be sure that the plastic is kept tight when nailing the frame material together.

2. Attach the hinges to the two braces and fasten the braces to the screen by fastening the hinges in place. Fasten each chain or rope to the frame or the screen with a large nail or screw. Drive a nail into each brace to serve as a tie-down point for the rope or nail. Adjust the shadow screen so

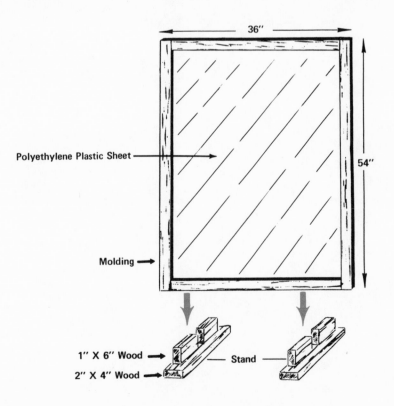

VERTICAL SHADOW SCREEN

that it tilts at a desirable angle, fasten the chain or ropes in place, and the shadow screen is ready to use.

Frosted Acetate: Slidecraft Co., Meadows A.V.C. Service.

VERTICAL SHADOW SCREEN

Another popular screen, the vertical shadow screen, is presented here as a variation of the basic design described in the instructions for making a slanting shadow screen.

Bulletin-Board Utilization

VIII

Many bulletin boards are not well planned or well executed, and therefore are not as effective in communicating to learners as they could be. By following a few simple suggestions, many teachers find that the bulletin board can be an effective teaching device.

General suggestions for constructing good bulletin boards, samples of layout design, ways of displaying three-dimensional objects on the bulletin board, and methods of attaching pictures and prints to the board without damage are presented in this chapter.

GUIDE LINES FOR BULLETIN-BOARD UTILIZATION

Although the ten suggestions listed here are not hard and fast rules, they are given in the hope that teachers will find them helpful in making bulletin boards more effective.

1. Plan the display around a central idea or theme.

2. Decide on the general design configuration, and sketch a layout on a sheet of paper (see Layout Designs, next in this chapter).

3. Keep the display simple; use a few well-chosen pictures rather than many. Too many pictures tend to make the display confusing.

4. Use an attention-getting headline or caption. Consider using a question or word-play in the caption; involve the viewer in what is presented.

5. Use lettering that can be seen easily and can be read at a distance.

6. Be sure the pictures or prints used are well-mounted.

7. Use a balanced arrangement (see Layout Designs, next in this chapter).

8. Use pins with colored heads to heighten interest.

9. Change the bulletin board frequently to keep interest high.

10. Involve students in planning and doing bulletin-board arrangement. Have students bring magazines from home containing useful pictures.

LAYOUT DESIGNS

The layout designs presented show the use of background shapes (usually cut from colored paper) the add interest, lines leading to centers of interest, balance in arrangement and the use of space for emphasis. Teachers should

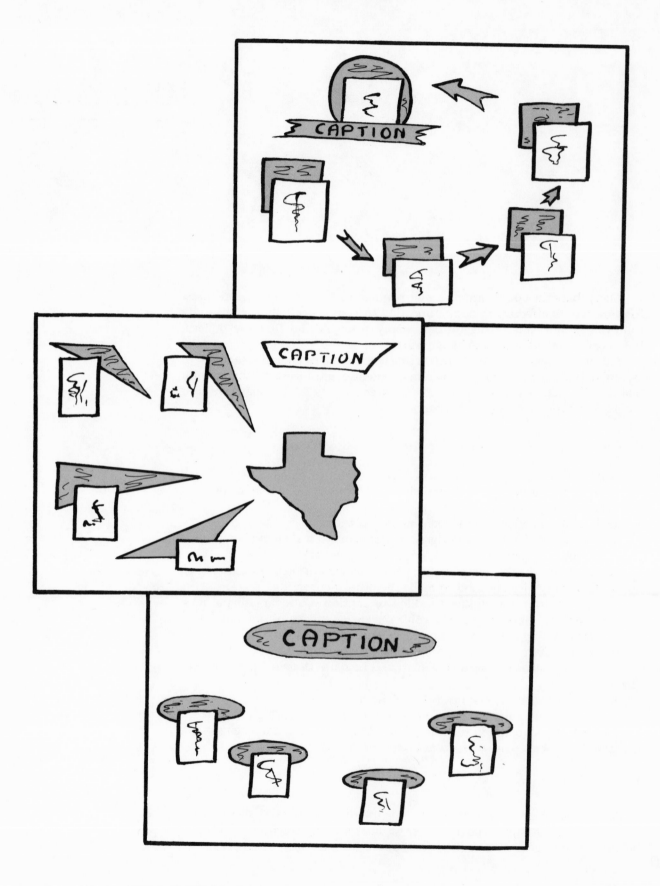

LAYOUT DESIGNS

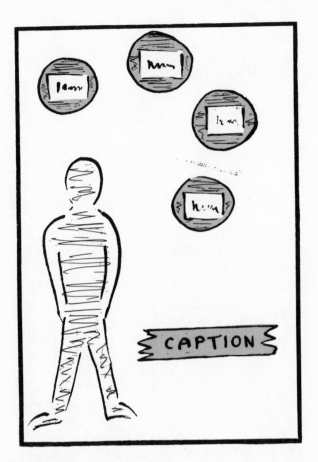

supplement the ideas presented here to help make the bulletin board an effective teaching device.

DISPLAYING THREE-DIMENSIONAL OBJECTS

Three-dimensional objects such as leaves, cloth samples, building materials, and other objects may often be attached directly to the bulletin board

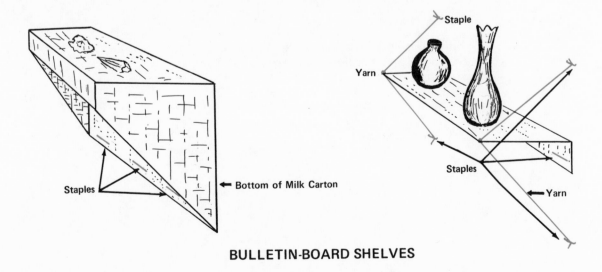

BULLETIN-BOARD SHELVES

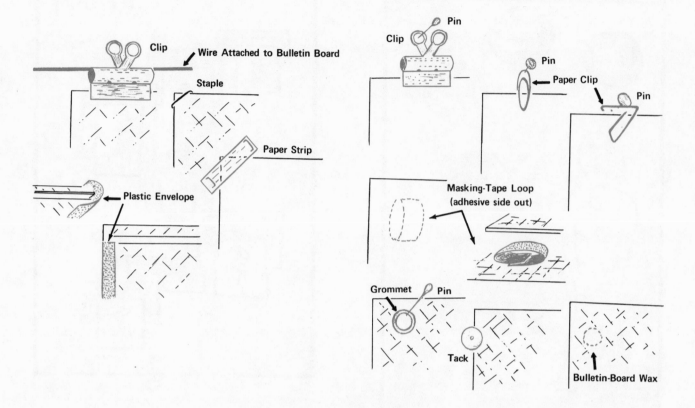

with staples, pins, or brads. Occasionally, small objects such as geological specimens, cultural artifacts, and small models can best be presented by placing them on shelves that have been attached to the bulletin board. Two shelf designs are presented that teachers have found useful and attractive.

ATTACHING PRINTS TO THE BULLETIN BOARD

Prints may be attached to the bulletin board without damage by following the accompanying illustrated suggestions.

Materials Sources

Bulletin-Board Wax: Lea Audio-Visual Service.
Masking Tape: Scotch-Brand Tapes, 3M Company.

Chalkboard and Charting Tools and Techniques

IX

By investing a little time in the preparation of basic chalkboard tools and techniques to fit specific instructional needs, the classroom teacher will be able to save time and be more effective in accurately presenting materials to the class. This chapter describes some chalkboard tools and techniques teachers have found useful in the past.

In this section four ways of using the chalkboard are described: chalkboard templates, chalkboard stencils, projected negative drawings, and the hidden chalkboard. In addition, there is a short discussion of special chalkboard inks. Two methods for enlarging drawings, applicable either to chalkboards or paper charts, are also presented; these are the grid method and the projection method.

TEMPLATES AND STENCILS

CHALKBOARD TEMPLATES

Chalkboard templates are outlines of basic shapes useful for quickly making uniform and accurate chalkboard drawings. Permanent templates are generally cut from plywood or masonite. Examples of subjects for template construction include various geometric shapes such as triangles, circles, parallelograms, and trapezoids; basic laboratory-equipment outlines, such as flasks, beakers, and burners; outlines of animals, plants, and the human body; shapes of states, countries, continents, or any other objects where there is an instructional need for repeated drawing with accuracy on the chalkboard.

Materials and Equipment

sharp pencil
carbon paper for outline transfer
drawing paper
masonite or plywood sheets larger than template size (cardboard for temporary templates)

CHALKBOARD TEMPLATES

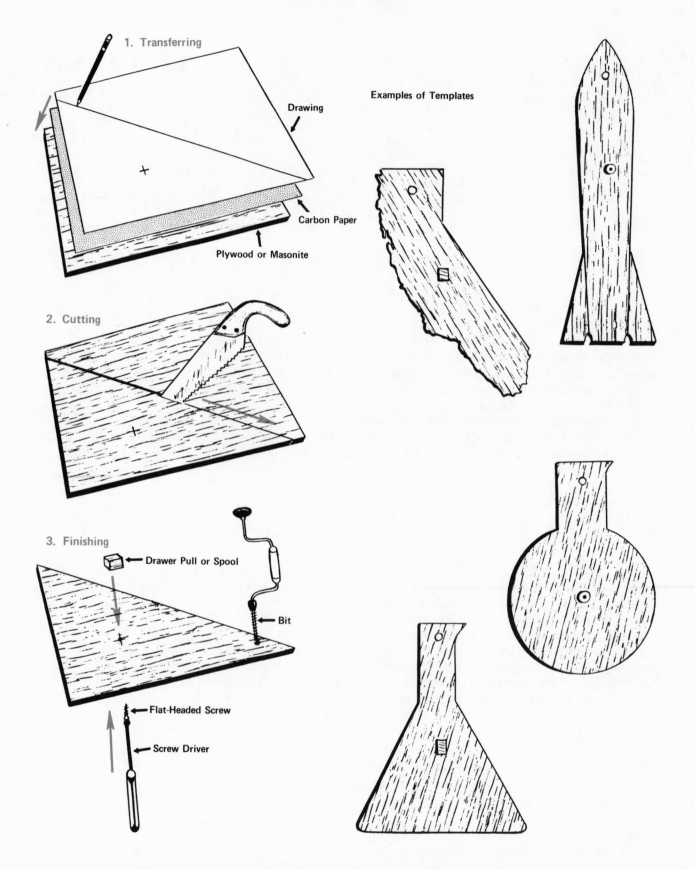

1. Transferring

Drawing

Carbon Paper

Plywood or Masonite

2. Cutting

3. Finishing

Drawer Pull or Spool

Bit

Flat-Headed Screw

Screw Driver

Examples of Templates

brace and bit or drill
drawer pull or empty thread spool
flat-headed wood screw
sandpaper
saw
scissors (to cut cardboard templates)

Procedure

1. Outline the desired shape in pencil on a sheet of paper. Using carbon paper, transfer the completed outline to a piece of cardboard (temporary template) or masonite or plywood (durable, permanent template).

2. Cut the shape from cardboard with scissors, or from plywood or masonite with a saw. To allow for the thickness of the chalk, cut any indentations larger than you wish to have them in the chalkboard drawing. Smooth off any rough edges with sandpaper.

3. Fasten a knob to the center of a plywood or masonite template so that you can hold it more firmly and easily in position on the board. Drawer pulls or empty spools work nicely for this purpose. Use glue or screws to fasten the knob in place, being sure to sink the head of the screw into the template so that the screw will not damage the chalkboard as the template is used. Two or three $3/4''$ squares of felt glued to the back of the template will keep it from slipping on the chalkboard when in use.

Drill a hole near one edge of the template, making the hole large enough to allow for hanging the template on a finish nail beneath the chalk tray. If templates are hung below the chalk and eraser tray, they will be readily available when needed.

Materials Source—(Commercially Prepared Templates)

Teaching Materials Service, 914 North Ave., Beloit, Wis. 53511.

CHALKBOARD STENCILS

Large chalkboard outlines may be easily made by the stencil method. Subjects used in the production of templates often lend themselves equally well to chalkboard reproduction through the use of this tool.

Materials and Equipment

a variety-store window shade (or a sheet of heavy paper or light cardboard)
pencil for outlining the stencil on the shade
leather spacer or hammer and saddle punch
board to place underneath the shade as perforations are made
3″-wide board, slightly longer than the window shade is wide
window-shade hangers and movable rack mounts for holding the board on the rack
chalk and an eraser

Procedure

Draw or trace the outline of the figure on the window shade. An opaque projector might be used in making the drawing by the method described later in this chapter. Then:

1. Use a leather spacer or a hammer and saddle punch to produce evenly spaced perforations along the outline previously drawn on the shade. Be sure to use a board underneath the drawing as perforations are made.

CHALKBOARD STENCILS

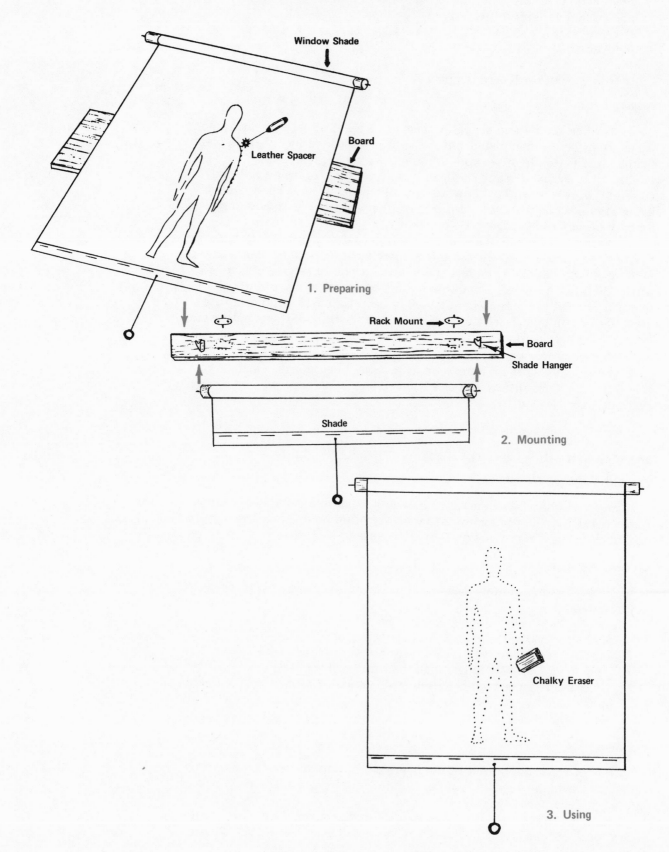

Window Shade

Board

Leather Spacer

1. Preparing

Rack Mount

Board

Shade Hanger

Shade

2. Mounting

Chalky Eraser

3. Using

2. Hold the stencil up to the light as progress is made to make sure that all holes are cleanly cut. Mount the board in the rack at the top of the chalkboard, fasten window-shade hangers to the board, and mount the window shade on the hangers as illustrated.

3. Pull the shade down, hold it against the chalkboard, and pat a chalk-covered eraser along the perforations. Release the window shade so that it will roll up.

Fill in the spaces between the chalk spots by quickly sketching over the dotted outline with a sharp piece of chalk. If additional identical outlines are needed, simply move the stencil along the rack to a new position and repeat the process. (*Note*: In some instances teachers may want to use heavy paper or cardboard in making stencils. The same basic procedure is used in preparing these materials for stencil production.)

Materials Source—(Commercially Prepared Stencils)

Corbett Chalkboard Stencils.

PROJECTED NEGATIVE DRAWINGS

A 2″ × 2″ slide in negative form, projected on the chalkboard, may be very useful as a basis for supplemental chalk drawings done from a projected

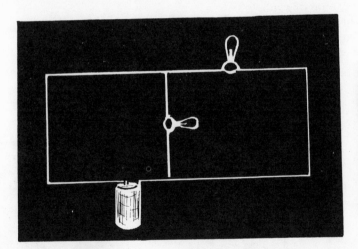

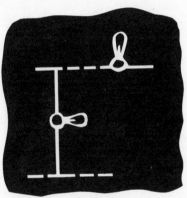

Supplemental Chalk Drawings

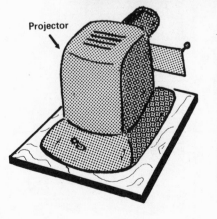

Projector

Electrical-Wiring Diagram
Projected Negative Image

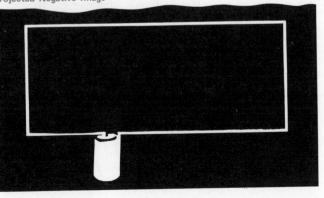

PROJECTED NEGATIVE DRAWINGS

schematic drawing or diagram. Drawings used in this way should be done on white paper with black ink, and should be photographically copied with a 35mm. camera. The film should be processed through the negative stage, and the negative should then be mounted between glass for projection. Negatives of this sort may be projected in a dimly lighted room. Teachers may add supplemental information to the projected image with chalk, and erase and modify as needed, while the slide is being projected in front of a class during a lesson presentation.

HIDDEN CHALKBOARD

Materials prepared in advance by the teacher or students will have special dramatic effect if it is hidden from view until needed to illustrate a point made in a discussion or report. Material prepared in advance may be hidden from view by the back of a map, or by a specially constructed movable curtain which hangs to one side of the chalkboard when not in use. The instructions and accompanying illustrations presented here are concerned with construction and hanging of a permanent curtain for a hidden board.

Materials and Equipment

cloth curtain, cut into two pieces, long enough to completely cover the chalkboard and board frame; (color should harmonize with color scheme of room)

split plastic rings or shower-curtain hooks to slide along the wire curtain support

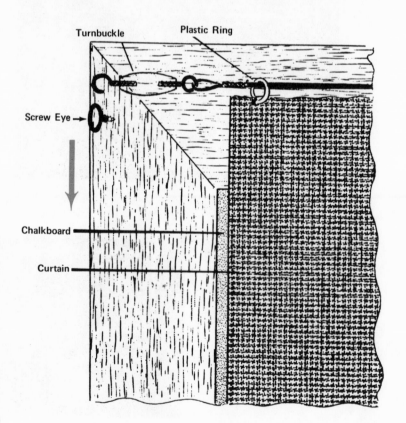

HIDDEN CHALKBOARD

strong wire slightly longer than the chalkboard and chalkboard frame
screw eyes to hold each end of the wire
one or two turnbuckles to tighten the wire

Procedure

Set the screw eyes into the frame above and slightly to one side of the chalkboard. Fasten the turnbuckle(s) to the end(s) of the wire. Sew the plastic rings to the curtain, spacing evenly. Thread the wire through the rings and hang. Attach a turnbuckle to one of the screw eyes, pull the wire tight, and fasten the other end of the wire (or the other turnbuckle) to the second screw eye. Tighten the turnbuckle(s) to pull the wire tight. The chalkboard curtain is now ready to use.

CHALKBOARD INKS

Many times teachers have a need for repeated use of basic materials put on the chalkboard. However, quite often these basic materials need to be altered from day to day because of additional material learned, changes in world conditions, changes in weather, or other new information. By the use of chalkboard inks, the teacher is able to place an outline on the chalkboard that cannot be accidentally erased and will allow for the addition and deletion of chalk-drawn materials without affecting the ink outline. Chalkboard inks are soluble and can be cleaned off with solvents at the conclusion of a unit of work.

Materials Source

Chalkboard Ink: Time-Saving Specialties.

ENLARGING DRAWINGS

The two processes described in this section are excellent methods of producing enlarged drawings on chalkboards or on charts. First the grid method is explained, then opaque projection drawings are discussed.

GRID METHOD

The grid method is used to enlarge small drawings on the chalkboard (or on charts) for use in lesson presentation. Teachers will find this technique very useful and practical. Little artistic skill is required to produce accurate, attractive drawings.

Materials and Equipment

sharp, soft lead pencil
ruler
yardstick
sharp chalk
eraser
picture to be transferred
poster board

Procedure

1. Using a ruler and soft lead pencil, draw a grid on the picture to be transferred; or to avoid damaging the picture, draw the grid on a sheet of tracing paper, place the tracing paper on the top of the drawing or print, and

THE GRID METHOD

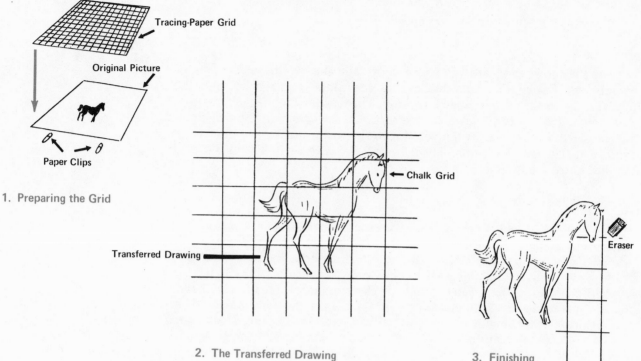

Tracing-Paper Grid

Original Picture

Paper Clips

1. Preparing the Grid

← Chalk Grid

Transferred Drawing ▬▬▬▬

Eraser

2. The Transferred Drawing

3. Finishing

fasten it into place with paper clips. The grid should have from 1/4" to 1" between lines, depending upon the size of the picture.

2. Using a yardstick and sharpened piece of chalk, draw a grid on the chalkboard (or chart) using a greater distance between lines; from 2" to 4" distance is usually required. Draw the picture on the enlarged grid, one square at a time, starting at one corner. The grid on the original picture serves as an excellent reference for accurate transfer of lines to the proper relative position within the larger chalk squares.

3. After the drawing is completed, remove the grid lines with an eraser and touch up your drawing "freehand," if desired. Very good results are usually achieved with this technique if teachers follow the steps outlined here.

PROJECTION METHOD

Many times teachers wish to enlarge small drawings or pictures for use in class discussion, but feel that they do not possess the necessary background in art techniques to create an acceptable chart or chalkboard enlargement. By using the projector, teachers with little artistic know-how can transfer pictures easily and accurately from books, slides, or filmstrips to chart or chalkboard.

Materials and Equipment

projector
suitable picture
sharp piece of white chalk (and additional colored pieces if needed)
pencil (plus other drawing instruments) for chart enlargements
poster board

OPAQUE PROJECTION DRAWING

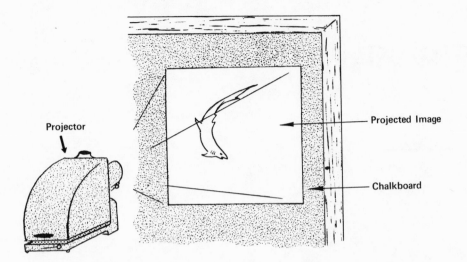

Projector

Projected Image

Chalkboard

Procedure

Place the picture, slide, or filmstrip in the projector, turn on the switch, and govern the size of the image on the chalkboard or chart by moving the machine toward or away from the board. To achieve a sharp focus, move the focusing lens into or out of the lens housing as needed. Using chalk (or pencil, in charting), outline the projected figure on the chalkboard (or chart).

As you progress toward completing the drawing, make periodic checks of your tracing to see if needed detail has been omitted from the chalkboard drawing. This check is easily accomplished by turning on the room lights, as the room lights will blot out the projected image, thus revealing any undrawn details. Continue tracing until your picture is complete.

Tape Recording for Instruction

X

The assumption is made that teachers using this manual can accomplish the necessary operations for the recording of sound on tape. However, tapes which accompany pictorial presentations such as opaque-projected pictures, slide sets, and study prints often need to include sound effects. Ways of duplicating tapes, duplicating disc recordings on tape, simultaneous recording of voice and music, and making sound effects are presented here.

COPYING RECORDED SOUND

TAPE DUPLICATION

An original tape, or portions of several tapes, may be duplicated easily if two tape recorders and an appropriate connecting cord (a cord with a male plug on each end) are available. An electrical company or school shop should be able to provide an appropriate cord for connecting the recorders. (*Illustration on page 169.*)

Materials and Equipment

two tape recorders
blank tape
original recording(s)
appropriate connecting cord (a cord with a male plug on each end)
sheet of paper and a pencil.

Procedure

Set up and turn on both tape recorders. Place the original tape on one of the machines, set the counter at 000, and begin playing the tape. As the tape is played, jot down the counter setting for the beginning and ending of various selections to be used in duplication; then, rewind the tape and reset the counter at 000. In duplication, use the references written on the sheet of paper to allow for quickly skipping over unwanted material by using the fast-forward speed on the tape recorder containing the original tape recording. Then:

1. Connect the two tape recorders by plugging one end of the connecting cord into the external speaker *output* of the tape recorder containing the

TAPE DUPLICATION

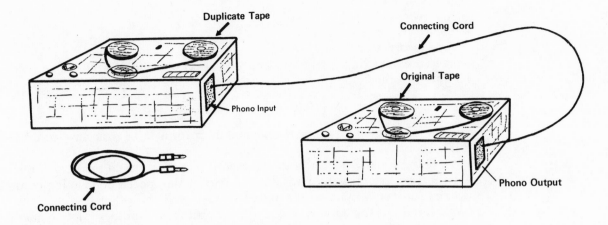

original tape, and plug the other end into the radio-phono *input* of the other tape recorder. Place a clean tape on the recorder to be used in recording the duplication.

2. Set the volume control on the machine containing the clean tape to about one-third of the full range, and press the *record* switch. Begin playing the original tape recording, and adjust the volume control on the machine containing the original until the record-level indicator on the machine doing the duplication is responding as desired.

3. Rewind the original tape, start the duplicating tape recorder, and then the recorder containing the original tape. Continue taping as desired.

DISC DUPLICATION ON TAPE

Selected readings, portions of musical works, and other materials on discs often need to be edited and pulled together from various sources in order to meet specific needs of certain situations. By using a tape recorder, record player, and special connecting cord (a cord prepared by a school shop or electrical company), a teacher may be able to construct a tape containing all the needed sections. (*Illustration below.*)

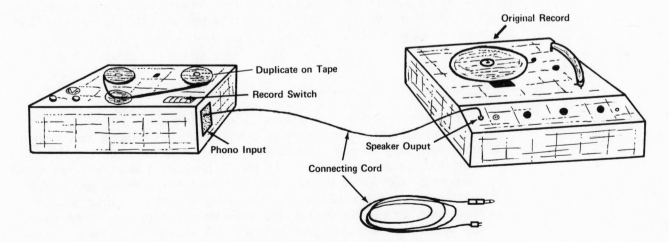

DISC DUPLICATION ON TAPE

blank tape
disc recording(s)
record player
tape recorder
special connecting cord (with Jones plug on one end and telephone jack
    on the other)

Procedure

Place all needed equipment and materials on a table near an electrical outlet. Then:

1. Plug in and turn on both the record player and tape recorder. Connect the two machines by plugging one end of the special connecting cord into the speaker output of the record player, and the other end into the phono input of the tape recorder (direct method). Another way to take sound from the record player may be used. With a cord which has alligator clips on one end and a plug on the other, attach the clips to the speaker terminals of the record player, and plug the other end of the cord into the phono input of the tape recorder (indirect method). Higher-fidelity recordings are possible using the *direct* method.

2. Place a disc on the turntable, adjust the tone-arm weight and the record speed, and make the correct needle selection. Turn the volume on the *tape recorder* up about one-third of the full range. Play the disc, adjusting the volume by turning the volume control on the *record player* until a desirable volume setting has been indicated on the tape-recorder volume indicator. Press the *record* switch on the tape recorder, and record the disc or portions thereof as desired.

TAPING RADIO AND TELEVISION SOUND

Often teachers have difficulty taping radio and television programs because of room noises or other interference in the area where the recording must be made. By using a connecting cord with alligator clips on one end and a male plug on the other, it is possible to record without picking up room noises. Attach the alligator clips to the speaker terminals of the radio or television speaker as illustrated immediately hereafter for the indirect method of simultaneous voice and record duplication, and plug the other end of the cord into the tape recorder. Turn on the record player, adjust the volume control until the desired volume is indicated on the tape-recorder volume indicator, and start recording when desired.

COMBINED RECORDINGS

SIMULTANEOUS RECORDING OF VOICE AND MUSIC

Dramatic renditions, oral interpretations, and spoken presentation to go with visual presentations such as slide sets, prints, art displays, and opaque projections may often be enhanced by appropriate narration with a well-selected musical accompaniment in the background. When planning sound tapes to go with visual presentations, write a script, allowing enough time between comments to allow for changes in projections where necessary. Music should be in the background while the narration is being presented, and should increase in volume between slide changes or other projection changes. Musical background should be continuous and smooth throughout the presentation to help give continuity and unity to the lesson presentation.

SIMULTANEOUS RECORDING OF VOICE AND MUSIC

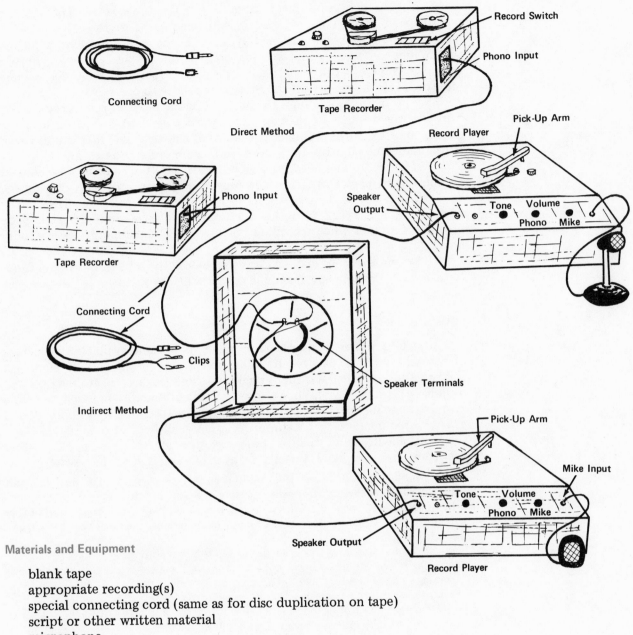

Materials and Equipment

blank tape
appropriate recording(s)
special connecting cord (same as for disc duplication on tape)
script or other written material
microphone
tape recorder
record player with microphone input jack

Procedure

Place all the needed materials on a table. Then:

1. Plug in and turn on the tape recorder and the record player. Connect the two machines by plugging one end of the special cord into the speaker output of the record player, and the other end into the phono input of the tape recorder (direct method). Another way to take sound from the record player may be used. With a cord which has alligator clips on one end and a plug on the other end, attach the clips to the speaker terminals of the record player, and plug the other end into the phono input of the tape recorder

(indirect method). Higher-fidelity recordings are possible using the *direct* method of connection.

2. Place a disc on the turntable, adjust the tone-arm weight and the record speed, and make the correct needle selection. Turn the volume on the *tape recorder* up about one-third of the full range. Play the disc, adjusting the volume by turning the volume control on the *record player* until a desirable volume setting has been indicated on the tape recorder volume indicator. Lift the needle off the record, and place to one side.

3. Plug the microphone into the microphone input of the *record player*. Turn up the volume control on the *record player* while talking into the microphone until the volume indicator on the tape recorder indicates an appropriate volume. Note the volume setting for voice and record.

4. If the recording is to begin with music, turn the *voice volume* control on the record player *off*, turn the tape recorder *on* and begin playing the disc. When voice is desired, turn the music volume *down*, turn the *voice* volume *up*, and speak into the microphone. The microphone should be turned off, except when recording the voice, to eliminate unnecessary room noises.

5. Several trial runs may be necessary before the tape is in finished form. With a little practice, professional results will be obtained by the average teacher.

SOUND EFFECTS

As small portable transistor tape recorders become available to teachers in our schools, it is possible for them to capture certain sounds, such as a train passing by, a car starting, or a jet airplane leaving the ground, as these sounds occur in real situations. However, it is often more practical to create sound effects for plays and dramatic recordings at school or at home. Sound effects listed here are easy to produce, sound realistic, and require no expensive equipment, other than a tape recorder and microphone. All other needed materials are readily available, usually at no cost to the teacher.

Airplane motor or electric saw. Hold electric hair clippers against mike, or hold a stiff piece of cardboard against the revolving blades of a fan.

Arrow in flight and impacting. Whip a willow branch or limber rod through the air near the mike; then strike the base of the branch or rod against the table near the mike to simulate impact.

Boat with motor. Run a popsicle stick back and forth over corrugated cardboard.

Boat being rowed. Alternate between blowing through a straw into a pan of water, and working a rusty hinge back and forth.

Chains rattling. Pour steel washers from one hand to another.

Fire. Crumple a sheet of cellophane; increase proximity to the fire by moving closer to the mike. Diminish intensity by moving away from the mike.

Gun shot. Place a pillow on a table, and strike sharply with a yardstick or ruler.

Horses' hooves. Drum fingers on an inverted cigar box placed over a mike. For a horse passing over a bridge, click clam shells together near mike.

Rain falling. Slowly roll a ball of cellophane between the hands.

Shutters in a storm. Follow working of a rusty hinge back and forth with impact of wood on wood.

Steamship whistle. Blow across a partially filled pop bottle.

Stream or brook. Blow lightly through a straw into a pan of water.

Surf. Roll dried beans back and forth in a cake pan.

Telephone voice. Hold a small can to one side of the face, with the opening toward the lips, while recording.

Thunder. Rattle a large, limber cookie sheet near the mike.

Train Engine. Rub the face of the mike over flannel clothing.

Waterfall. Roll cellophane or tissue paper between hands.

Recommended Readings, Films, and Filmstrips

SELECTED TEXTS

Leading text books containing information concerning the philosophy and psychology involved in utilization of instructional materials, as well as basic research information, utilization principles, and a basic understanding of new communication media applications to instruction are included in this list.

A-V Instruction: *Materials and Methods*, 3rd ed., by James Brown, Richard Lewis, and Fred Harcleroad. New York: McGraw-Hill Book Company, Inc.

Audio-Visual Methods in Teaching, 3rd ed., By Edgar Dale. New York: Holt, Rinehart, and Winston, Inc.

Audio-Visual Materials, *Their Nature and Use*, 3rd ed., by Walter Wittich and Charles Schuller. New York: Harper and Row.

Planning and Producing Audiovisual Materials, 2nd ed., By Jerrold E. Kemp. Scranton: Chandler Publishing Company.

Teaching and Media: *A Systematic Approach*, by Vernon S. Gerlach and Donald P. Ely. Englewood Cliffs: Prentice-Hall, Inc.

Techniques for Producing Visual Instructional Media, by Ed Minor and Harvey R. Fry. New York: McGraw-Hill Book Company.

Using Audio-Visual Materials in Education, by James S. Kinder. New York: American Book Company.

SELECTED MATERIALS-PREPARATION BOOKS

Art-work Size Standards for Projected Visuals. Rochester: Eastman Kodak Co. (pamphlet S-12; free)

Better Mounting by the Dry Mount Method. Derby, Conn.: Seal, Inc.

Charting Statistics, by Mary Spear. New York: McGraw-Hill Book Co.

Classroom Cartoons for All Occasions, by Jerome C. Brown. Belmont: Fearon Publishers.

Creative Teaching with Tape. St. Paul: Revere-Mincom Division, 3M Company.

Graphic Presentation, by Frances J. McHugh. Holyoke: Tecnifax Corporation.

Graphic Science. New York: Graphic Science (9 Maiden Lane, 10038).

Graphics Handbook, by Ken Garland. New York: Van Nostrand Reinhold Company.

Handbook of Graphic Presentation, by Calvin F. Schmid. New York: Ronald Press.

The How to Do It Booklet of Tape Recording. St. Paul: 3M Company.

How to Use a Tape Recorder, by Dick Hodgson and H. J. Bullen. New York: Hastings House.

Instant Artwork—Kodak Compass. Rochester: Eastman Kodak Co. (publication P-1-63-1; free)

Learning with the Overhead Projector, by Arthur E. Ring and William J. Shelley. Scranton: Chandler Publishing Company.

Legibility Standards for Projected Materials. Rochester: Eastman Kodak Co. (pamphlet S-4; free)

Lettering Techniques, by Martha F. Meeks. Austin: Visual Instruction Bureau, University of Texas.

Magnetic Sound Recording for Motion Pictures. Rochester: Eastman Kodak Co. (publication P-26)

Making the Most of Charts, by K. W. Haemer. Holyoke: Tecnifax Corporation.

Modern Graphic Arts Paste-up, by Gerald A. Silver. Chicago: American Technical Society.

Paper Bag Puppets, by De Atna M. Williams. Belmont: Fearon Publishers.

Paste-up Drafting—Kodak Compass. Rochester: Eastman Kodak Co. (publication P-1-64-1; free)

Pictographs and Graphs, by Rudolf Modley and Dyno Lowenstein. New York: Harper and Row.

Radio and Television Sound Effects, by Robert B. Turnbull. New York: Holt, Rinehart, and Winston.

Reproduction Methods for Business and Industry. New York: NPD Corporation. (monthly journal).

Simplified Techniques for Preparing Visual Instructional Materials, by Ed Minor. New York: McGraw-Hill Book Co.

The Tape Recorder, by Robert Sloan, Jr. Austin: Visual Instruction Bureau, University of Texas.

Tape Tips from Capital Audio Engineers. Los Angeles: Capital Recordings.

Technical Presentations, by John Bateson. Holyoke: Tecnifax Corporation.

The Technique of the Sound Studio, by Alec Nisbett. New York: Hastings House.

SELECTED INSTRUCTIONAL-PLANNING BOOKS

For teachers who need assistance in general instructional planning the books listed here are most helpful.

Instructional Design: A Plan for Unit and Course Development, by Jerrold E. Kemp. Belmont: Fearon Publishers.

Individualization of Instruction, by Virgil M. Howes. New York: The Macmillan Company.

Preparing Instructional Objectives, by Robert F. Mager. Belmont: Fearon Publishers.

SELECTED EQUIPMENT-OPERATION MANUALS

Leading audio-visual equipment operation manuals are listed here for teachers who need help in learning to operate equipment or who need to refine skills previously developed.

A B C's of Audio-Visual Equipment and the School Projectionist's Manual, by Philip Mannino. State College, Pa.: M. O. Publishers.

Audiovisual Machines, by Raymond L. Davidson. Scranton: Intext Educational Publishers.

A-V Instructional Materials Manual, by James W. Brown and Richard B. Lewis. New York: McGraw-Hill Book Company.

Mediaware: Selection, Operation, and Maintenance, by Raymond Wyman. Dubuque: William C. Brown Company.

Operating Audio-Visual Equipment, 2nd ed., by Sidney C. Eboch, San Francisco: Chandler Publishing Company.

SELECTED FILMS

A number of 16mm films which give supplemental information concerning techniques for preparing materials are listed below.

A B C of Puppet Making, I and II. Hollywood, Calif.: Bailey Films, Inc.

Better Bulletin Boards. Bloomington: Indiana University Films.

Bulletin Boards: An Effective Teaching Device. Hollywood, Calif.: Bailey Films, Inc.

Chalkboard Utilization. New York: McGraw-Hill Book Company.
Creating Cartoons. Hollywood, Calif.: Bailey Films, Inc.
Dry Mounting Instructional Materials. A series. Iowa City: University of Iowa. (*Basic Techniques, Cloth Backing, Display and Use, Laminating and Lifting, Special Techniques*)
Dry Mount Your Teaching Pictures. New York: McGraw-Hill Book Company.
The Felt Board in Teaching. Detroit: A-V Production Center, Wayne State University.
Flannel Boards and How to Use Them. Hollywood, Calif.: Bailey Films, Inc.
Handmade Materials for Projection. Bloomington: Indiana University Films.
How to Do Cartoons. Trenton: Samuel Lawrence Schulman Productions.
How to Make and Use a Diorama. New York: McGraw-Hill Book Company.
Lettering Instructional Materials. Bloomington: Indiana University Films.
Magazines to Transparencies. Tallahassee: Audio-Visual Center, University of Florida.
Tape Recording for Instruction. Bloomington: Indiana University Films.
Wet Mounting Instructional Materials. Bloomington: Indiana University Films.

The following series of 8mm single-concept films showing materials-preparation techniques is available for use with either standard 8mm or super-8mm projectors. These films are very useful for learning centers and in individual instruction. At this writing, distribution arrangements are in transition. Orders or inquiries may be sent to:

McGraw-Hill Book Company, Text-Film Division, Box 404, Hightstown, N. J. 08625.

If the McGraw-Hill Book Company cannot supply, inquiries may be sent to:

Chandler Publishing Company, Oak and Pawnee Streets, Scranton, Pennsylvania 18515.

Dry Mounting (Press)
Dry Mounting (Hand Iron)
Permanent Rubber Cement Mounting
Mounting: A Two-Page Picture
Mounting: A Cut-Out Picture
Mounting: Overcoming Dry Mounting Problems
Mounting: Using Laminating Film
Cloth Mounting (Roll)
Cloth Mounting (Fold) Part I
Cloth Mounting (Fold) Part II
Mounting: Setting Grommets
Lettering: The Felt Pen (Basic Skills)
Lettering: The Felt Pen (Applications)
Lettering: Prepared Letters
Lettering: Wricoprint

Lettering: Wricosignmaker
Lettering: Leroy 500 and Smaller
Lettering: Leroy 700 and Larger
Transparencies: Handmade Method
Transparencies: Heat Process
Transparencies: Principle of Diazo Process
Transparencies: Diazo Process
Transparencies: Spirit Duplicator
Transparencies: Picture Transfer I
Transparencies: Picture Transfer II
Transparencies: Making Overlays
Transparencies: Adding Color
Transparencies: Mounting and Masking
The Spirit Duplicator: Preparing Masters
The Spirit Duplicator: Operation

SELECTED FILMSTRIPS

Diorama as a Teaching Aid. Teaching Aids Laboratory, Ohio State University.
Embedding Specimens in Plastic. Syracuse: Syracuse University Films.
Handmade Lantern Slides. Columbus, Ohio: Teaching Aids Laboratory, Ohio State University.
How to Keep Your Bulletin Board Alive. Columbus, Ohio: Teaching Aids Laboratory, Ohio State University.
Make Your Chalk Teach. Detroit: Wayne State University A-V Production Center.
Making Geographical Models. Columbus, Ohio: Teaching Aids Laboratory, Ohio State University.
Mounting Pictures. Austin, Texas: Visual Instruction Bureau, University of Texas.
The Opaque Projector. Columbus, Ohio: Teaching Aids Laboratory, Ohio State University.
Using Charts and Graphs in Teaching. Pasadena, California: Basic Skill Films, Inc.

Materials
Sources

Ansco Films, GAF Corporation, 140 W. 51st St., New York, N. Y. 10020.
Artype, Inc., 345 E. Terra Cotta Ave. (Rte. 176), Crystal Lake, Ill. 60014.

Beckley-Cardy Company, 1900 N. Narragansett Ave., Chicago, Ill. 60639.
Bell & Howell, Inc., 6800 McCormick Rd., Chicago, Ill. 60645.
Charles Beseler Company, 219 S. 18th St., East Orange, N. J. 07018.
Bourges, Inc., 80 Fifth Ave., New York, N. Y. 10011.
Arthur Brown & Bro., Inc., 2 W. 46th St., New York, N. Y. 10036.

Carlo's, 220 Fifth Ave., New York, N. Y. 10001.
Carr Corporation, Cleveland, Ohio 44115.
Castolite Company, Woodstock, Ill., 60098.
Chart-Pak, Inc., 1 River Rd., Leeds, Mass. 01053.
Cling-Tite Letters, 866 N. Wabash Ave., Chicago, Ill. 60611.
Copease Company, 425 Park Ave., New York, N. Y. 10022.
Corbett Chalkboard Stencils, 548 Third Ave., North, Pelham, N. Y. 10065.
Craftint Manufacturing Co., 18501 Euclid Ave., Cleveland, Ohio 44112.
Cushman and Denison Manufacturing Company, 625 Eighth Ave., New York, N. Y. 10018.
Eugene Dietzgen Co., 2425 N. Sheffield Ave., Chicago, Ill. 60614.
Ditto Division, Bell & Howell, 6800 McCormich Rd., Chicago, Ill. 60645.
Dorfman Products, 23813 Archwood St., Canoga Park, Calif. 91304.
Dymo Products Co., P. O. Box 1030, Berkeley, Calif., 94701.

Eastman Kodak Co., 343 State St., Rochester, N. Y. 14650.
Esterbrook Pen Co., Box 230, Cherry Hill, N. J. 08034.
Ronald Eyrich, 1091 N. 48th St., Milwaukee, Wisc. 53208.

Glassoloid Corporation of America, 32 Wellington Ave., Clifton, N. J. 07011.
H. T. Herbert Co., 2121 41st Ave., Long Island City, N. Y. 11101.
Hernard Manufacturing Co., Executive Boulevard, Elmsford, N. Y. 10523.
Hillary Co., 141 Hillary Circle, New Rochelle, N. Y. 10804.
Horder's, 231 Jefferson St., Chicago, Ill. 60606.
Instructo Products, Paoli, Pennsylvania 19301.

Johnson Plastics (E-Z-I Film), 526 Pine St., Elizabeth, N. J. 07206.
Judy Co., 310 N. Second St., Minneapolis, Minn. 55401.
Keuffel and Esser Co., 20 Whippany Rd., Morristown, N. J. 07960.
Koh-i-Noor, Inc., 100 North St., Bloomsbury, N. J. 00804.
Krengel Manufacturing Co., 227 Fulton St., New York, N. Y. 10007.

Labelon Tape Co., 10 Chapin St., Canandaigua, N. Y. 14424.
Lea Audio-Visual Service, 240 Audley Dr., Sun Prairie, Wisc. 53590.

Lewis Artist Supply Co., 6408 Woodward Ave., Detroit, Mich. 48202.

Mach-A-Tach, 26 E. Pearson St., Chicago, Ill. 60611.

Maggie Magnetic, Inc., 39 W. 32nd St., New York, N. Y. 10001.

Magnet Sales Co., 3955 S. Vermont Ave., Los Angeles, Calif. 90037.

Major Services, 1740 W. Columbia Ave., Chicago, Ill. 60626.

Manhattan Wood Letter Co., 151 W. 18th St., New York, N. Y. 10011.

Marsh Stencil Co., 707 E. B St., Belleville, Ill. 62222.

Minnesota Mining and Manufacturing Co. (3M Company), Box 3100, St. Paul, Minn. 55101.

Mitten's Designer Letters, P. O. Box 351, Redlands, Calif., 92373.

Multi-Plastics Co., Box 316, 7332 Deering Ave., Northridge, Calif. 91324.

Ohio Flock-Cote Co., 13229 Shaw Ave., East Cleveland, Ohio 44112.

Oravisual Co., Inc., Box 11150, St. Petersburg, Fla. 33733.

Ozalid Division, General Aniline and Film, 140 W. 51st St., New York, N. Y. 10020.

Para-Tone, Inc., P. O. Box 136, LaGrange, Ill. 60525.

Polaroid Corp., 549 Technology Square, Cambridge, Mass. 02139.

Prestype, Inc., 194 Veterans Blvd., Carlstadt, N. J. 07072.

Program Aids Co., Inc., 550 Fifth Ave., New York, N. Y. 10036.

Redikut Letter Co., 12617 S. Prairie Ave., Hawthorne, Calif. 90250.

Seal, Inc., Roosevelt Dr., Derby, Conn. 06418.

Slidecraft Co., Meadows A.V.C. Service, Mountain Lakes, N. J. 07046.

W. S. Stensgaard and Associates, 30 Rockefeller Plaza, New York, N. Y. 10020.

Stenso Lettering Co., 1101 E. 25th St., Baltimore, Md. 21218.

Tablet & Ticket Co., 1021 W. Adams St., Chicago, Ill. 60607.

Techni-Craft, P. O. Box 1024, Petersburg, Va. 23803.

Tecnifax Corporation, 195 Appleton St., Holyoke, Mass. 01040.

3M Company, Box 3100, St. Paul, Minn. 55101.

Time-Saving Specialties, 2922 Bryant Avenue, South, Minneapolis, Minn. 55408.

Transilwrap Co., 4427 N. Clark St., Chicago, Ill. 60640.

Transograph Co., 1 River Rd., Leeds, Mass. 01053.

Uniline Corporation, 33450 Western Ave., Union City, Calif. 94587.

Ward's Natural Science Establishment, P. O. Box 1712, Rochester, N. Y. 14603.

Wood-Regan Instrument Co., 184 Franklin Ave., Nutley, N. J. 07110.

Index of
Topics
and
Illustrations